# ADVANCE PRAISE

"In his newest book, John DiJulius brings his customer service expertise to bear on the question of relationships. How can we build better relationships with our customers that will keep them coming back for more? DiJulius offers a smart prescription that builds on traits you already have—empathy, vulnerability, hospitality, and authenticity—which will deepen your relationships not only with customers but also with family and friends, old and new."

**—DANIEL PINK,** author of *When, Drive,* and *To Sell Is Human*

"Every day, consumers are telling us what's important to them: convenience, service, attention, empathy. Even in a digital age, personal relationships are critical to building trust and loyalty. This well-researched book will provide the inspiration to not simply connect with your customers but also to build real human connections."

**—RICH KRAMER,** Chairman, CEO, and President, The Goodyear Tire & Rubber Company

"If true customer and employee loyalty is what you are looking for, *The Relationship Economy* will help you and your team build a genuine human connection and improve the impact this connection has on brand experience in the digital age."

—**LISA LUTOFF-PERLO,** President and CEO, Celebrity Cruises

"I believe each of us can be classified as either a giver or a taker. John DiJulius' latest is a must-read; it blares out to all leaders the importance of human interconnectivity at all levels within the organization. Human connectivity creates understanding, which in turn develops empathy, respect, trust, and thriving, growing relationships among leaders, employees, and customers."

—**REAR ADMIRAL TOM LYNCH,** United States Navy, (ret.)
Chairman, NewDay USA

# THE
# RELATIONSHIP
# ECONOMY

## BUILDING STRONGER
## CUSTOMER CONNECTIONS
## IN THE DIGITAL AGE

# JOHN R.
# DIJULIUS III

GREENLEAF
BOOK GROUP PRESS

Published by Greenleaf Book Group Press
Austin, Texas
www.gbgpress.com

Distributed by Greenleaf Book Group

For ordering information or special discounts for bulk purchases, please contact Greenleaf Book Group at PO Box 91869, Austin, TX 78709, 512.891.6100.

Design and composition by Greenleaf Book Group and Kim Lance
Cover design by Greenleaf Book Group and Kim Lance

Publisher's Cataloging-in-Publication data is available.

Print ISBN: 978-1-62634-643-7

eBook ISBN: 978-1-62634-644-4

Part of the Tree Neutral® program, which offsets the number of trees consumed in the production and printing of this book by taking proactive steps, such as planting trees in direct proportion to the number of trees used: www.treeneutral.com

Printed in the United States of America on acid-free paper

19 20 21 22 23 24 25    11 10 9 8 7 6 5 4 3 2

First Edition

# ALSO BY JOHN R. DIJULIUS III

*Secret Service: Hidden Systems That Deliver
Unforgettable Customer Service* (Amacom, 2003)

*What's the Secret? To Providing a World-Class Customer
Experience* (Wiley, 2008)

*The Customer Service Revolution: Overthrow
Conventional Business, Inspire Employees,
and Change the World* (Greenleaf, 2015)

*The Best Customer Service Quotes Ever Said* (Greenleaf, 2016)

*To my wonderful family, Claudia, Johnni, Cal, and Bo,*
*each of you inspires me to be a better person every day.*
*Thank you for all the love and support you have given me.*
*I am the luckiest person in the world.*

# CONTENTS

# WELCOME TO
# THE RELATIONSHIP ECONOMY

> *"Today's illiterate are those who have an inability
> to truly make a deep connection with others."*

S ince I was old enough to remember, my life's obsession was to play shortstop for the Cleveland Indians. I worked at it. I was committed and passionate, and nothing was going to stop me. Except for maybe the lack of a little talent or, in my case, the lack of a lot of talent. No matter how hard I worked, there was absolutely no way I was ever going to play in the big leagues. There are certain genetic skills we are either born with or not. And if not, there is not much we can do about it.

There are skills we can develop, however, and of all these, there is one that when mastered will, without question, have the biggest impact on us personally and professionally.

> There is one that when mastered will, without question, have the biggest impact on us personally and professionally. That skill is the ability to build an instant connection with others.

That skill is the ability to build an instant connection with others. This is way more than a mere communications skill. It is the ability to communicate with a purpose—to build your community at every stage of your life. Building a relationship with someone else, whether an acquaintance, friend, customer, coworker, or a total stranger, is far and away the most important skill every human being should be taught at an early age and then should hone throughout life. This skill should be taught at home, in school from pre-kindergarten to graduate school, and, of course, in business. Unfortunately it is rarely taught in any formal way.

## The Lost Art of Building Rapport

Today we are living in the "digital disruption era." Technology has provided us with unprecedented advances, information, knowledge, instant access, and entertainment. We have computers, mobile phones, tablets, the internet, social media, apps, and artificial intelligence—assistants like Siri and Alexa, chatbots, virtual concierges, facial recognition, and self-driving cars.

However, as convenient as these advances make our lives, they also have changed the way we communicate, behave, and think and have led to a dramatic decline in our people skills. As a society we are now relationship disadvantaged. We no longer become curious about others or eager to engage in conversations. The younger generation primarily communicates electronically, and the explosion of ecommerce means we go out less and less. In business, multi-channel communication has dramatically reduced phone calls to companies; customers can get answers and place orders via email, on websites, or through social media channels.

The pendulum has swung over to high tech and low touch. Consequently we long for a sense of community, belonging, and purpose, a world in which people actually know our name, what we do, what is important to us, and have trust in one another. Today trust is an endangered value. Those who understand that human touch is the most important part of any experience—especially a great customer experience—will flourish. Personally and professionally, success is increasingly about creating and building human connections.

> Those who understand that human touch is the most important part of a great customer experience will flourish. Success is increasingly about creating and building human connections.

## The Benefits of Strong Connections

When you have the ability to make an instant connection, get people to instantly like you, make them feel comfortable, and fully develop relationships of all kinds, you are likely to have more fulfillment and success. I cannot think of anything that will give you a bigger advantage in all aspects of your life—that includes higher self-esteem, a larger network, greater support system, and more resources. Your personal and professional life will be filled with an abundance of people who think highly of you, love you, and have your back.

People who have key relationships and positive influences in their life are usually less stressed because they have someone they can talk to, vent to, and confide in when life gets tough. And it is just as rewarding to be a positive influencer for others—to have others rely on you.

Lives can be changed for the better because the right friendships can make a difference in someone's life at a critical point. In an interview with Tom Bilyeu on his series *Impact Theory*, author Simon Sinek said, "Those relationships that we foster over the course of a lifetime . . . will oftentimes save your life. They will save you from depression. They will save you from giving up, they will save you from any matter of negative feelings about your capabilities, your own future, when someone just says I love you and I will follow you no matter what."[1]

People with strong relationships have a greater potential for more professional success, are less impacted by corporate politics, laugh more, and experience less depression. Research has shown that social engagement and meaningful relationships are associated with living a longer life and improving your overall health.[2] The flip side is also true: Julianne Holt-Lunstad, the lead author of a study that reviewed and analyzed research in this area, noted, "A lack of social relationships was equivalent to smoking up to 15 cigarettes a day."[3]

Studies have repeatedly shown that the happiest people are the ones with the most meaningful relationships.[4] Yet it seems to have become increasingly difficult to maintain these relationships. Too often we are guilty of treating the people we come in contact with as part of a transaction or as a private audience for us. We miss out on an opportunity to make a deeper connection that can potentially enrich both lives.

> A lack of social relationships was equivalent to smoking up to 15 cigarettes a day.

Think about your best friend or your significant other; both were strangers at one time. How different your life would be if they had remained strangers. Thank goodness you found a way to develop a rapport that turned an initial contact into a lifelong relationship.

But something is happening in our society. Research shows that over the past several decades our inner circle—the people we trust the most—is much smaller than in the past. Today the average American trusts only 10 to 20 people.[5]

## Relationships Are More Vital Than Ever in the Business World

Understand this: There is an Uber coming to every industry. Uber is part of the digital disruption that completely turned the taxi and limousine industries upside down. But you can track similar developments in other realms. Amazon has disrupted nearly all retail businesses—grocery stores, health insurance, banks, home security, entertainment, pharmacies, and shipping, and it continues to expand into other fields. Airbnb has disrupted the hotel industry. Netflix wiped out video rental stores.

> In the past, cutting-edge innovation had a much longer shelf life in overcoming competition. Now, however, many of your competitors can replicate your innovations and quickly reduce any temporary advantage you had in the market.

No business is safe. In the past, cutting-edge innovation had a much longer shelf life in overcoming competition. Now, however, many of your competitors can replicate your innovations and quickly reduce any temporary advantage you had in the market. The answer cannot just be about technology, either. To be sure, technological advancements are critical to every business staying relevant. However, technology by itself is not a differentiator. The more you place technology between the company and the customer, the more you remove the human experience.

People crave human interaction. Customers desire recognition and a personalized experience; technology can never be empathetic or build relationships. In short, technology cannot provide genuine hospitality. It cannot express empathy, make people feel cared for, express emotions and vulnerability in a relatable way, or make people smile and laugh.

For anyone and any business to thrive in the future, they will have to master the art of relationship building.

> *"Our careers, our companies, our relationships,*
> *and indeed our very lives succeed or fail, gradually,*
> *then suddenly, one conversation at a time."*
> —SUSAN SCOTT[6]

## A Relationship-Building Strategy

It takes a great deal of work to build deep, long-term relationships. In Ben Healy's article "How to Make Friends, According to Science," he shared a recent study that found it takes approximately 50 hours of socializing to go from acquaintance to casual friend, an additional 40 hours to become a "real" friend, and a total of 200 hours to become a *close* friend. "Self-disclosure makes us more likable, and as a bonus, we are more inclined to like those to whom we have bared our soul. Longing for closeness and connection is universal," Healy said.[7]

A study by the Relational Capital Group revealed that 89 percent of senior leaders believe that relationships are the most important factor in their success year over year. However, the study also revealed that only 24 percent of these leaders actually do anything intentionally to promote building those relationships. Finally, the study further indicated that less than 5 percent of organizations actually have any specific strategies for helping their professionals develop and strengthen the relationships required to achieve their goals.[8]

> A study revealed that 89 percent of senior leaders believe that relationships are the most important factor in their success . . . only 24 percent of these leaders actually do anything intentionally to promote building those relationships . . . less than 5 percent of organizations actually have any specific strategies for helping their professionals develop and strengthen the relationships required to achieve their goals.

## What It Takes to Master Rapport Building

No one is born with a rapport-building gene. And not everyone is inclined to be outgoing or to strike up a conversation with people they don't know. The environment you grow up in plays a big part in how you act. If you had extremely outgoing parents, chances are you will grow up to behave similarly. However, even if you were not exposed to an outgoing environment in your early years, this skill set can certainly be developed and mastered. There are certain sets of characteristics you need to work on in order to master relationship building. We will be discussing them in more detail in the following chapters. But briefly, to develop strong relationships you:

- Must be authentic
- Must be obsessively curious
- Must be a great listener
- Must have incredible empathy
- Must love people

## MUST BE AUTHENTIC

People have great BS detectors. Your interest in others and your desire to make a connection must be authentic. If you are asking questions merely for appearances, just to make a sale, or to turn the conversation back to yourself, people will see through you. Not being authentic will earn you a poor reputation. You are much better served simply coming out and asking for what you want; people will respect you more. Instead of trying to manipulate people into buying products or services, you must show them you care. You need to demonstrate that you are genuinely interested in others and that you realize they are human beings with a life and not just customers you are trying to sell to.

## MUST BE OBSESSIVELY CURIOUS

Those who are the strongest at relationship building are extremely curious. They are dying to learn about others and their experiences. They are curious not only about subjects that interest them but also about unfamiliar subjects. They become investigative reporters, wanting to learn as much as possible about other people's lives and passions. They truly enjoy learning; they explore what makes human beings tick.

## MUST BE A GREAT LISTENER

There is a lot more to being a good listener than just letting the other person talk. You need to be attentive, patient, make good eye contact, not interrupt, ask probing questions, and finally pause to process what you heard before responding.

## MUST HAVE INCREDIBLE EMPATHY

One of our strongest human talents is the ability to empathize with another person's situation. Seeing and understanding someone's experience from their perspective, walking in their shoes, is key.

## MUST LOVE PEOPLE

No two people are alike. No one is perfect. Everyone is flawed. Yet everyone has unlimited potential. Human beings are incredible. Everyone has a story about their life journey—what they have overcome, their accomplishments, their incredible talents, fears, regrets, and dreams. Each human being has a story inside. The fun is discovering those incredible stories. When you truly serve people, your goal is not to make money or to get them to do what you want, but to take care of their needs and desires.

> Each human being has a story inside. The fun is discovering those incredible stories. When you truly serve people, your goal is not to make money or to get them to do what you want, but to take care of their needs and desires.

# The Customer Service Revolution 2.0

*The Relationship Economy* is the follow-up to my groundbreaking book, *The Customer Service Revolution*. In that book I explained that creating a customer service revolution means:

> A radical overthrow of conventional business mentality designed to transform what employees and customers experience. This shift produces a culture that permeates into people's personal lives, at home,

and in the community, which in turn provides the business with higher sales, morale, and brand loyalty—making price irrelevant.

In other words, the customer service revolution is about having a fanatical obsession to deliver the best possible customer experience, making it your single biggest competitive advantage. Revolutionary companies create "experience epiphanies" that fill a gap customers never knew existed. Since technological advancements have come at the expense of human connections, organizations now need to reinvent their business model to marry digital and human experiences in the best way possible.

> Since technological advancements have come at the expense of human connections, organizations now need to reinvent their business model to marry digital and human experiences in the best way possible.

## Why the Relationship Economy, Why Now?

In the past 25 years I have built three successful businesses, including one of the top customer service consulting firms that works with incredible companies—The Ritz-Carlton, Lexus, Starbucks, Chick-fil-A, Celebrity Cruises, and many more—and I have seen a seismic shift happening today. Technology is changing the world, and not always for the better. For all the benefits it is bringing to businesses, it is coming at a significant cost. The cost is weaker human relationships that are vital to customer experiences, employee experiences, and happiness. Focusing strictly on a digital experience will eliminate customer loyalty and emotional connection to a brand, which is why the Relationship Economy is emerging. Business leaders around the world have to take advantage of technology advancements while balancing a human experience that people crave, want, and need.

## What Is the Relationship Economy?

In a Relationship Economy the primary currency is made up of the connections and trust among customers, employees, and vendors that create significantly more value in what we sell. These relationships and connections help make price irrelevant.

> In a Relationship Economy the primary currency is made up of the connections and trust among customers, employees, and vendors that create significantly more value in what we sell. These relationships and connections help make price irrelevant.

The Relationship Economy is about building a culture that recognizes the importance of each individual and of making everyone a part of a community that is working toward something bigger—a community that makes them feel cared for.

The Relationship Economy is how strongly you feel about  the people and businesses in your life. Relationships are the biggest differentiator in customer and brand loyalty. Relationships are at the center of all we do.

The chapters that follow explore in depth what a Relationship Economy is, why it's important, and how to dominate in it.

> The Relationship Economy is about building a culture that recognizes the importance of each individual and of making everyone a part of a community that is working toward something bigger—a community that makes them feel cared for.

Chapter 2 examines the rapid pace at which business and customer service are changing, like no other time in history.

Chapter 3 explores ways to humanize the experience, and chapter 4 delves into the new reality of the touch-screen world we are living in today.

Chapter 5 lays out a systematic approach to building instant rapport with others personally and professionally; chapter 6 shows how businesses are executing those principles in their organizations.

Chapters 7 and 8 look at the benefits of strong relationships between your business and your customers, and your business and your employees.

Chapter 9 shows how you can be the Uber of your industry; chapter 10 emphasizes the importance of the micro experiences to customer loyalty; and, in conclusion, chapter 11 puts it all into the broader context of a meaningful life.

You need to make your entire organization relationship-centric from the inside out. Customers don't recommend businesses they like; they recommend businesses they *love*. When you accomplish that, you make you and your brand competitor-proof and irreplaceable.

> *"With the advancement in technology, it is ironic that the disruptive force happening today in business is relationship building."*

## CHAPTER 1 TAKEAWAYS

- Today's illiterate are those who have an inability to connect with others.

- The greatest skill that has the biggest impact on us, personally and professionally, is the ability to build an instant connection with others.

- Today we are living in the "digital disruption era." Technology has provided us with unprecedented advances. It has also changed the way we communicate, behave, and think and has led to a dramatic decline in our people skills. As a society we are now relationship disadvantaged.

- Studies have repeatedly shown that the happiest people are the ones with the most meaningful relationships.

- In the past, cutting-edge innovation had a much longer shelf life in overcoming competition. Now, however, many of your competitors can replicate your innovations and quickly reduce any temporary advantage you had in the market.

- For anyone and any business to thrive in the future, they will have to master the art of relationship building.

- Eighty-nine percent of senior leaders believe that relationships are the most important factor in their success . . . only 24 percent of these leaders actually do anything intentionally to promote building those relationships. Less than 5 percent of organizations actually have any specific strategies for helping their professionals develop and strengthen the relationships required to achieve their goals.

- To master rapport building, you

  - Must be authentic
  - Must be obsessively curious
  - Must be a great listener
  - Must have incredible empathy
  - Must love people

- Since technological advancements have come at the expense of human connections, organizations now need to reinvent their business model to marry digital and human experiences in the best way possible.

- There is a seismic shift happening today. Technology is changing the world, and not always for the better. For all the benefits it is bringing to businesses, it is coming at a significant cost: weaker human relationships that are vital to customer experiences, employee experiences, and happiness.

- The Relationship Economy is about building a culture that recognizes the importance of each individual and making everyone a part of a community that is working toward something bigger—a community that makes them feel cared for.

# STATE OF SERVICE

> *"The world is becoming a little less human, and that has a cost.*
> *So it's time for leaders in the business world to think about how*
> *they can recognize the benefits of technology while also accepting*
> *its limitations. Leaders need to consider how they can get back*
> *to a more human approach to business that acknowledges our*
> *universal need for interaction and understanding."*[1]
>
> —DAN SCHAWBEL

Before we begin to work on how to thrive in the Relationship Economy, it's important to assess where we are and how we got that way. To start with, recognizing the role that technology has played is paramount.

Tom Peters, for example, in his book *The Excellence Dividend*, refers to the advancement of technology as the Tech Tsunami. He notes "there is a larger threat looming, one that has been

> There is a larger threat looming, one that has been building for a long time, and which, over the next five to fifteen or twenty years, is likely going to knock us back on our heels with once-in-a-century consequences.

building for a long time, and which, over the next five to fifteen or twenty years, is likely going to knock us back on our heels with once-in-a-century consequences. It's not globalization. It's not immigration. It's technology."[2]

He's not alone in that assessment. The World Economic Forum released a report predicting that by 2025, there will be more machines in the workforce than humans.[3] And it is not only blue-collar jobs that are threatened. For the first time in history, white-collar professionals are in danger as well. An Oxford University analysis claims that, in the next two decades, nearly 50 percent of American white-collar jobs will be at risk, either to automation or artificial intelligence (AI). As Daniel Huttenlocher, dean of Cornell Tech, has written, "The industrial revolution was about augmenting and replacing physical labor, and the digital revolution has been about augmenting and replacing mental labor."[4]

> By 2025, there will be more machines in the workforce than humans. In the next two decades, nearly 50 percent of American white-collar jobs will be at risk, either to automation or artificial intelligence (AI).

## The Rise of Robo Restaurants

One perhaps surprising field that has taken advantage of the shift to technology is the restaurant industry, where a shortage of available workers has driven up costs and limited the ability of some restaurants to open additional locations. Spyce, a casual fast-food place begun by four MIT graduates, is set on opening the first truly robotic restaurant chain in the US. Its founders say the robots help improve consistency and speed and prepare food in three minutes or less, while enabling the company to serve its food at reasonable prices.[5]

Another example is the Chinese restaurant chain Haidilao, which has partnered with Panasonic to open up a fully automated kitchen in Beijing. The new establishment will feature robots that take orders and prepare and deliver raw meat and fresh vegetables to customers to put into soups prepared at their tables. The automated kitchen will reportedly be used to help Haidilao expand to as many as 5,000 locations around the world.[6]

## Need Reservations? There Is an App for That

You needn't go all the way to a robotic kitchen to encounter AI in the food world. When commanded, Google Duplex will call a restaurant and make reservations. The software is very advanced, with a realistic human voice that mimics the "uhhs" and "umms" typical of most conversations. It's undoubtedly a harbinger of things to come, as this software could easily expand to booking appointments for other businesses such as hair salons, doctors' offices, and hotels.

Another feature of Google's Duplex and its AI capabilities across the globe is the possibility of eliminating language barriers. "There's the opportunity to [give people] the ability to call a business in a country where [they] don't speak the language," says Nick Fox, Google's vice president of product and design. "I'd be able to speak to the assistant in a language that I speak and then it could speak to the business in a language that makes sense to them. That's a really interesting way this system can be used to break language barriers."[7]

The applications of AI are just beginning to be explored. In fact, Servion predicts that AI will power 95 percent of all customer interactions by 2025 and will do it so effectively that customers will not be able to "spot the bot."[8]

## Technological Disruption and Dislocation

There is no arguing that machines and AI are faster, cheaper, more efficient, and make fewer mistakes than humans. When a bank started using chatbots to handle more than 1.5 million claim requests each year, it found that the work of 85 bots was equal to the output of 200 full-time human employees at only 30 percent of the cost.[9] As for the future, Juniper Research predicts that chatbot conversations will be responsible for cost savings of more than $8 billion per year by 2022, up from $20 million in 2017.[10]

But what are some of the implications of these sweeping technological shifts? One result is the commoditization of professional knowledge. For decades, professionals were able to charge premium fees for their expertise, which was considered a rare and valuable skill. As a result of living in a world with access to the internet, the value of expertise in many professions has been dramatically reduced. Much of what customers would have called an expert for in the past—in private banking, consulting, or even engineering, say—can be found online in a few minutes today.[11]

This raises the question: How can professionals differentiate themselves? The marketplace is flooded with companies offering the same products, and it is nearly impossible to tell any of them apart. I believe that today the only way a company can differentiate itself is through building relationships with its employees, customers, and the community.

I repeat: Technology is not the answer. Even the most highly developed machines cannot show genuine compassion and empathy or recognize customer pain points on a personal level. AI cannot engage humans emotionally. The most important asset needed to truly connect with customers is the ability to empathize, yet AI solutions are incapable of placing themselves in another person's shoes. It is time to make the human part of the customer experience our top priority.

In their book *Race Against the Machine*, Erik Brynjolfsson and Andrew McAfee say, "The root of our problems is not that we're in a Great Recession or a Great Stagnation, but rather that we are in the early throes of a Great Restructuring. Our technologies are racing ahead, but our skills and organizations are lagging behind."[12]

> **Our technologies are racing ahead, but our skills and organizations are lagging behind.**

Businesses have created this situation for themselves by not focusing on the customer experience, not making it a priority, and not training customer-facing employees how to connect with customers. Yes, this is a crisis; but it's also a potential turning point: Organizations and professionals can complain, or they can adapt to what the future holds.

## How Are You Going to Compete?

The best place to start is to change the old thinking paradigm that got us here. Customer service and soft skills are not common sense. People are not born with them. The quality of your organization's customer service comes down to one thing and one thing only: the service aptitude of every employee you have. It's the most critical component in building a world-class customer experience culture.

> *Service Aptitude: A person's ability to recognize opportunities to meet and exceed customers' expectations, regardless of the circumstances.*

Service aptitude does not apply to the technical or operational side of the experience, which is also a critical part of a company's customer service. Service aptitude represents the hospitality side only, how an employee makes another person feel.

## Why Employees Lack Customer Empathy

The most important thing a leader needs to know is that the vast majority of employees have extremely low service aptitude, especially when they are just entering the workforce. There are several reasons for this:

- Your employees do not know what "world-class" is. For most frontline employees, their standard of living typically does not afford them the opportunity to fly first class, stay at five-star resorts, drive a luxury automobile, and enjoy other high-end experiences. Yet we, as managers, expect those same employees to be able to deliver world-class service to clients, guests, patients, or customers who may be accustomed to it. It doesn't make any sense.

- Your employees are not your customers. In the vast majority of businesses, customer-facing employees cannot relate to their customer. They do not share the same age range, income, or professional position. Many businesses have frontline employees in their twenties dealing with clients between the ages of 35 and 50; maids who live in modest homes but clean customers' residences worth many thousands or millions; or account executives, accountants, lawyers, consultants, and other professional service providers who deal directly with CEOs and top entrepreneurs.

- Your employees are not looking at a situation from the customer's perspective. Remember, many employees have never been their own customer, have never needed the services and products their company provides, and cannot comprehend what the customer's mind-set is. Therefore, they find it difficult to empathize, be compassionate, and anticipate a customer's needs. World-class service organizations respond by teaching their employees to view things from the customer's perspective. Businesses need to focus on that point of view, instead of their own perspective. They must understand what the customer actually experiences at each interaction point with the organization.

- As a business you compare yourself to the rest of your industry, which is a mistake. Whether you are a law firm, insurance agent, jewelry store, or accounting firm, any comparison to your competition is really pointless. Your firm's client doesn't hang up with you and call another accounting firm. After your customers deal with you, they interact with businesses in completely different industries. They finish their errands, go to the dry cleaner, go shopping, and encounter other enterprises. As a result, they either wish the other businesses were as good as yours, or vice versa.

- Your employees work on autopilot. All businesses battle with employees who simply go through the motions, from time to time even becoming insensitive to their customers. While consulting with a large hospital, I found out that too often the nurses and doctors would refer to patients as "201B," saying something like "201B needs their medicine." They were referring to a room and a bed number, instead of an actual person. Hardly a recipe for a good patient experience.

In order to dominate in the Relationship Economy, organizations have to intentionally train their employees to avoid the traps of a low service aptitude and embrace the customer's perspective. Doing that requires real commitment on the part of a company and someone to make sure that it's followed up by action.

> *"It is not the employees' responsibility to have a high service aptitude; it is the company's job to teach it to them."*

## The One Thing the Best Customer Experience Companies Do Differently

Nearly every business states how important customer service is to them. However, the vast majority don't truly mean it, are not willing to do what it takes, and will never be a world-class customer service organization. I can tell which companies are the pretenders and which are legit by asking just one simple question, "Who is in charge of your company's customer experience?" A contact center supervisor or director of your customer service team does not qualify.

> I can tell which companies are the pretenders and which are legit by asking just one simple question: "Who is in charge of your company's customer experience?"

The roles of Chief eXperience Officer (CXO) or Chief Customer Officer (CCO) have been two of the fastest-growing executive positions for the past decade, but too often these are empty titles. The majority of companies do not have anyone who *owns* their customer experience, who loses sleep at night over how the company is treating customers. Companies have heads of operations, marketing, accounting, sales, and human resources, but rarely do they have someone in charge of their second biggest asset (after employees). And that asset is the customer.

Companies need truly senior-level executive sponsorship and a commitment to the long-term strategy of dominating their industry by providing superior customer service. I am talking about a leader who oversees the entire company's customer service—every department. That person should not be the president, CEO, or owner, but someone who reports directly to them.

## Becoming a Customer-Obsessed Organization

The emphasis on customer service is not a purely altruistic exercise. Leaders love to talk about revenue streams by showing graphs and charts with a breakdown of sales by categories. Of course, it is important to know the percentage of sales generated by products or services and to monitor trends, especially the growth or decline of your business revenue. However, there is one critical component that every business has in common, which is never discussed: 100 percent of your sales come from one place—your customers!

> **100 percent of your sales come from one place—your customers!**

Similarly, executive leaders frequently focus on analyzing the company's profit and loss to determine where the company is overspending and being wasteful and then figure out how to reduce expenses to drive more profit to the bottom line. However, once again, the company's biggest expense does not show on your P&L, at least not directly. There is no line item for poor customer service, but nothing may have a greater impact on your bottom line than dissatisfied customers. Poor customer service dramatically causes loss of sales, decline of company reputation, lack of new customers and referrals, an increase in returns and refunds, increased discounting, more service recovery, higher advertising expenses, lower morale, higher turnover, increased hiring, and more training—which further perpetuates a poor customer experience. It is imperative that every person in your company understands that your biggest expense is dissatisfied customers.

It's clear that developing a customer-obsessed organization extends well beyond your customer service team. It has to be the responsibility of every single department: human resources, training, marketing, support, sales, IT, finance, operations, and most important, leadership. Employee compensation needs to be as focused on customer retention—delivering world-class customer service—as it is on customer acquisition.

A great example of how this might work is the sales commission plan for HubSpot, a marketing and sales software company based in Cambridge, Massachusetts. "In 2015, a sales rep earned commission on everything they closed," says Brian Halligan, CEO of HubSpot. "Now, we've made two important tweaks to it: a carrot and a stick. The stick was very unpopular. If a sales rep closed an account, and that account cancelled within eight months, the company would 'claw back' that commission. Painful, but effective. The carrot was easier, and also effective. The sales reps that do the best job at setting expectations, who have high retention rates and the happiest customers, receive a kicker, getting paid at a higher rate. Our sales reps are focused not only on closing customers, but on delighting customers."[13]

# What Has a Better ROI—Investing in Advertising or Customer Service?

When it comes to a company's budget, every department annually fights for an increase in its own budget. That's not surprising; the outcome will determine what the department is allowed to spend for the following year. This is especially true of the budgets for advertising versus customer service training. The only way to win the battle is to prove which expenditures will produce a better return on investment (ROI) for the company. The fact that this is even still a debate is a sign of old paradigm thinking by too many senior executives. A shortsighted obsession with constantly bringing in new customers to your business is significantly more expensive than building an incredible customer experience.

In *Our Social Times* article titled "Can Online Customer Service Deliver a Higher ROI than Marketing?" Tom Eggemeier, EVP Global Sales at Genesys, says that global budget expenditures on marketing and advertising were $500 billion a year compared to $9 billion spent on customer service. How does your company compare to that percentage?[14]

Start asking yourself if you are constantly offering incentives to "New Customers Only." What about rewarding the customers who have been loyal to your business for years—those who do business with you regularly, no questions asked, and refer others to your firm? You ignore them at your peril.

It is a fact that:

- Repeat customers spend more than new customers.

- Repeat customers give higher satisfaction scores.

- Repeat customers give referrals more often than new customers.

- You need five new customers to produce as much as one repeat customer.

In a study titled *The ROI from Marketing to Existing Online Customers,* published by Adobe, it was reported:

- A 5 percent increase in customer satisfaction can increase a company's profitability by 75 percent.
- 80 percent of your company's future revenue will come from just 20 percent of your existing customer base.[15]

Companies spend millions creating and advertising their brands, yet the customer's experience is what truly drives customer perception, retention, and referrals. If you take really good care of your existing clients, they will generate more new customers than any advertising campaign ever could. Think about what might happen if you reversed your budgets for advertising and customer service.

> Companies spend millions creating and advertising their brands, yet the customer's experience is what truly drives customer perception, retention, and referrals. Think about what might happen if you reversed your budgets for advertising and customer service.

In any case, it is no longer acceptable to allow customer experience and marketing to act as separate silos. Both departments need to work together; otherwise the customer loses, which means ultimately the company loses. How do you merge marketing into the customer-experience hierarchy? Start by figuring out who owns the voice of the customer, initiate customer satisfaction surveys, sponsor soft-skill experiential training, and designate a senior executive to hold all departments and locations accountable for Key Performance Indicators (KPIs).

## Customer Experience Is the New Branding

Branding has changed. It is no longer about building a perception in your customer's mind. In the age of smartphones and social media, customer experience is the new branding. Customers are defining the brand to the business and everyone else, and we can find out what a large percentage of them think about any brand within minutes by simply searching Google.

Brands put billions into boosting awareness, satisfaction, and loyalty, but they often overlook the most powerful driver of customer value—emotional connection. Research shows that consumers who are emotionally connected with a brand are anywhere from 25 to 100 percent more valuable in terms of revenue and profitability than those who are "merely" highly satisfied with it.[16]

## Marketing Will Report to Customer Experience

Marketing is no longer in control of the brand, and revolutionary companies are acknowledging that by beginning to place the marketing department under customer experience. Within the next 5 to 10 years, that will be the norm. Now, if you are a chief marketing officer or head of your marketing department, don't panic. You have time to acquire the knowledge and training you need to smoothly make the transition to the chief experience officer who will oversee marketing.

According to the "Customer Experience Management Market,"

> Marketing is no longer in control of the brand, and revolutionary companies are acknowledging that by beginning to place the marketing department under customer experience.

a report by Grand View Research , the Customer Experience Management (CEM) market is estimated to grow from $5 billion to $13.18 billion by 2021. The major factors driving the CEM market include an increasing need to manage the customer experience throughout the customer journey, the need to retain customers, and competitive differentiation.[17]

Similarly, Forrester Consulting's white paper titled "The Business Impact of Investing in Experience" shows through research how businesses are being forced to make bigger investments in their customer experience. "Customer experience has quickly moved from competitive differentiator to business imperative. In a world where the answer to almost any question is at our fingertips, where AI is becoming a part of everyday life, and where we can get a week's worth of groceries delivered to our homes in less than an hour, consumers and business buyers have come to expect highly contextual and personalized experiences," noted the authors of the paper.[18]

> Customer experience has quickly moved from competitive differentiator to business imperative. In a world where the answer to almost any question is at our fingertips, where AI is becoming a part of everyday life, and where we can get a week's worth of groceries delivered to our homes in less than an hour, consumers and business buyers have come to expect highly contextual and personalized experiences.

Traditional "branding" is an old paradigm. Companies that are tired of spending an exorbitant amount of money on advertising and marketing are now reallocating those dollars toward customer experience training. The top customer service companies typically spend the least in their industries in advertising and marketing. They're proving that the new budget priorities are the direction of the future.

There's no denying that technology has amazing advantages to make it easier for the customer in most cases, provided businesses do it in moderation and not at the cost of the human experience. The new paradigm starts with hiring employees who genuinely like people and want to serve, then giving them the training that will increase their service aptitude, making sure there's a leader with the power to oversee and strengthen customer service across all departments, and allocating the budget to make it happen.

> *"We have to leverage our humanity, our ability to become better at connecting and collaborating with others, which will give ourselves the best chance of success in a rapidly changing world."*

## CHAPTER 2 TAKEAWAYS

- The world is becoming a little less human at a significant cost.

- By 2025 there will be more machines in the workforce than humans.

- AI will power 95 percent of all customer interactions by 2025.

- Another major implication of these sweeping technological shifts is the commoditization of professional knowledge. In the next two decades, nearly 50 percent of American white-collar jobs will be at risk, either to automation or artificial intelligence (AI).

- The quality of your organization's customer service comes down to one thing and one thing only: the service aptitude of every employee you have.

- In order to dominate in the Relationship Economy, organizations have to intentionally train their employees to avoid the traps of a low service aptitude and embrace the customer's perspective. Doing that requires real commitment on the part of a company and someone to make sure that it's followed up by action.

- The one thing the best customer experience companies do differently is have an executive leading their customer experience, i.e. a Chief eXperience Officer.

- Companies spend millions creating and advertising their brands, yet the customer's experience is what truly drives customer perception, retention, and referrals. Think about what might happen if you reversed your budgets for advertising and customer service.

- Revolutionary companies are beginning to place the marketing department under customer experience.

- There's no denying that technology has amazing advantages to make it easier for the customer in most cases, provided businesses do this in moderation and not at the cost of the human experience.

# HUMANIZING OUR FUTURE

> *"In the digital revolution, excellent human interaction skills become a premium advantage."*

As became obvious in the previous chapter, technological innovations and the rise of artificial intelligence (AI) have caused tremendous dislocations in today's workplace. But the best customer service companies recognize the competitive opportunity of using technology to perform basic jobs, enabling employees to focus on what is most important: building relationships that result in higher customer loyalty, retention, lifetime value, and job satisfaction.

Unfortunately the obsession with advancements in technology by many businesses has subconsciously sent the wrong message to employees: that success is about technological bells and whistles—websites, apps, social media, virtual tours, one click, iPads, kiosks, AI, and self-checkouts. As a result, employees have started using the technology as a crutch, thinking they themselves have less importance, less of a role in the overall customer experience. We need to reverse that assumption and reeducate employees that technology is just 10 percent of the customer experience and employees are 90 percent.

Facebook found out the hard way that implementing technology by itself is not the answer. In 2017 the social media giant tried having chatbots solely handle users' requests in the Messenger app. Unfortunately the bots failed to fulfill requests 70 percent of the time when deployed alone. Facebook eventually incorporated a combination of chatbots and human agents.[1]

## The Future of Customer Experience

Being able to build true sustainable relationships is the biggest competitive advantage in a world where automation, artificial intelligence, and machine learning are eliminating millions of jobs and disrupting entire industries, businesses, and careers. In the digital revolution, human interaction, compassion, empathy, and communication skills become a premium advantage.

> The most memorable customer experiences are the ones where an emotional connection was made, where both customer and employee felt something.

With the increase in the digitization and automation of customer interactions, your employees must be focusing on building relationships with customers. The most memorable customer experiences are the ones where an emotional connection was made, where both customer and employee felt something.

Eivind Jonassen, CEO of Omnicus, a technology company serving contact centers, describes how businesses should evolve. "You should reinvent and transform your organization from both a digital *and* human perspective. Only by combining the strengths of digital interfaces and humans can your organization hope to achieve its highest customer service objectives and goals."[2]

Kristin Smaby underscores that approach in her article, "Being Human Is Good Business." She says, "In an era when companies see online support as a way to shield themselves from costly interactions with their customers, it's time to consider an entirely different approach: building human-centric customer service through great people and clever technology. So, get to know your customers. Humanize them. Humanize yourself."[3]

> It's time to consider an entirely different approach: building human-centric customer service through great people and clever technology. So, get to know your customers. Humanize them. Humanize yourself.

## High Tech Meets High Touch

The Relationship Economy is a critical necessity in a world of digital disruption as companies try to figure out the new reality of human and machine interactions in designing their customer experience.

One thing that needs to stay a priority in this evolution is keeping the customer at the center of all your decisions. "With the pace and stresses of most lives, people want to pass along their emotional burden to another human, one they trust understands their needs and will work to resolve an issue," says Joshua Feast, the CEO of Cogito, an AI and behavioral analytics company.[4]

We are all social creatures and innately need relationships. The businesses that work at knowing their client as a person—with a family, concerns, and dreams—will be the ones who dominate their industries.

As Richard Shapiro notes in his book *The Endangered Customer*, "The human spirit can't be separated from human transactions and interactions—nor should it be. Customers do not want their lives

> The human spirit can't be separated from human transactions and interactions—nor should it be. Customers do not want their lives filled with endless robotic encounters. As automated transactions become faster, easier, and more reliable, making the human connection will become increasingly rare—and therefore increasingly more valuable.

filled with endless robotic encounters. As automated transactions become faster, easier, and more reliable, making the human connection will become increasingly rare—and therefore increasingly more valuable."[5]

He adds, "Those companies that will continue to deliver personalized service will create and sustain relationships that will positively impact bottom-line revenues and profitability. Organizations can meet these new challenges by employing technology that can be used to enhance, not diminish, the relationship."[6]

## Surviving in an Amazon World

E-commerce and the rise of mobile devices may have permanently changed the retail industry, but traditional retail was already tired, stale, and literally disappearing. Many of these businesses have historically provided a poor experience. Harris Interactive reports that customer service associates fail to answer a customer's questions 50 percent of the time. It's part of a vicious circle. As revenue declines, so does service, as more salespeople are cut and fewer are in stores to help customers.[7]

Nevertheless, brick-and-mortar retailers have an advantage that they should leverage. In an article titled "Surviving and Thriving in an Amazon World," retail consultant Roger Simpson said, "Where I see a massive advantage for brick and mortar stores is in the basic human need to interact with another human. This won't happen on Amazon, even with Alexa. Store team members can create a positive interpersonal experience that can't EVER be created online. This is one key advantage over Amazon and other online retailers, which needs to be exploited to its utmost."[8]

In other words, in order to compete, it comes back to relationships—building strong, solid, trusting relationships based on emotional connection, compassion, and empathy. Obviously, though, this all depends on having employees whose skills are adapted to the Relationship Economy.

> Where I see a massive advantage for brick and mortar stores is in the basic human need to interact with another human... Store team members can create a positive interpersonal experience that can't EVER be created online. This is one key advantage over Amazon and other online retailers, which needs to be exploited to its utmost.

## Digital Intelligence Up, Emotional Intelligence Down

Unfortunately that is not always the case. Because of the digital revolution, many members of the younger generations lack the necessary people skills of previous generations. Yet they are now leading start-ups that have developed quickly into leading companies. This will only accelerate the growing number of relationship-disadvantaged businesses.

In a TED Talk, hospitality entrepreneur Chip Conley addressed this phenomenon: "I believe looking at the modern workplace, the trade agreement of our times is opening up these intergenerational pipelines of wisdom so that we can all learn from each other. Almost 40 percent of us in the US workforce have a boss that is younger than

> And yet we expect these young digital leaders to somehow miraculously embody the relationship wisdoms we older workers have had decades to learn. It's hard to microwave your emotional intelligence.

us and that number is growing quickly. Power is cascading to the young like never before because of our increasing reliance on digital intelligence. We are seeing young founders of companies in their early 20s scaling them up to global giants by the time they get to 30. And yet we expect these young digital leaders to somehow miraculously embody the relationship wisdoms we older workers have had decades to learn. It's hard to microwave your emotional intelligence."[9]

> *"Investing in technology without investment in your people is a waste of time."*
> —ROGER SIMPSON[10]

## Traits for Effective Interactions

So where to begin? You can start by looking for employees predisposed toward a high level of customer service. Consider, for example, these seven key traits that lead to effective interactions.

### 1. Compassion and Empathy

Compassion is the ability to feel for another living being, which results in a desire to help. Having strong empathy for a customer's situation means seeing and understanding it from their perspective—walking in their shoes.

## 2. Engagement and Warmth

An employee with these traits is obviously happy in what they do and welcoming to the person they are doing it for. They seek eye contact, smile, and immediately put customers at ease by being friendly, cheerful, and caring.

## 3. A Drive to Serve

The employee is purposeful about focusing on the experience of the person they are serving above anything else.

## 4. Ownership

Ownership implies acting with the same care and thoughtfulness as an owner of the company and doing whatever it takes to ensure that customers leave happy with their experience.

## 5. Charitable Assumption

It's important to act as if no customer has bad intentions. After all, you do not want to punish 98 percent of your customers for what you are afraid the remaining 2 percent might do.

## 6. Presence

Effective employees cannot work on autopilot. Instead they are always fully in the moment, focused 100 percent on the person they are interacting with.

## 7. The Desire to Exceed Expectations

Those with a drive to go above and beyond are constantly looking for ways to surprise and delight customers.

## Social Skills = Job Security

As head of the world's largest professional-networking site, LinkedIn CEO Jeff Weiner knows better than anyone what companies are looking for in recruiting new talent. According to Weiner, careers involving social interaction and social skills will be most coveted and secure in our automated future. "As powerful as AI will ultimately become and is becoming, we're still a ways away from computers being able to replicate and replace human interaction and human touch. So there's a wonderful incentive for people to develop these skills because those jobs are going to be more stable for a longer period of time," says Weiner.[11]

> The ability to convince others that your ideas matter is the single greatest skill that will give you a competitive edge at a time when the combined forces of globalization, automation, and artificial intelligence trigger a wave of anxiety across every profession in every country.

Among the most valuable social skills is the gift of persuasion. Carmine Gallo, in his book *Five Stars: The Communication Secrets to Get from Good to Great*, emphasizes, "The ability to convince others that your ideas matter is the single greatest skill that will give you a competitive edge at a time when the combined forces of globalization, automation, and artificial intelligence trigger a wave of anxiety across every profession in every country. In the next decade, your ideas—and the ability to articulate those ideas successfully—will count more than ever. Persuaders are irreplaceable. If you can persuade, inspire, and ignite the imagination of others, you will be unstoppable, irresistible, and irreplaceable."[12]

Not everyone is born with the ability to make strong connections. That's a gift. But there are certain fundamental skills that everyone can learn. And it is incumbent on businesses to make them a mandatory part of customer service training. The most basic expression of warmth is simple, yet it is extremely hard to find in the real world today. I'm referring to a smile.

## Are Smiles Really Free?

Building rapport with customers starts with a genuine smile. Think of how many times you have heard, "A smile is free. It costs absolutely nothing to give but can mean the world to the person who receives it." I agree with the second part: It can mean the world to the person who receives it. But I do not agree that a smile always costs absolutely nothing. From a personal standpoint, yes, it costs us nothing to smile at one another. In business, however, it takes a lot more than reminders to get a large group of people constantly smiling. To get all your employees to do that comes at a significant cost to both the business and customers.

Think about the friendliest businesses you deal with, those where it would be hard to find an employee who isn't smiling—for example, Disney, The Ritz-Carlton, Southwest Airlines, or Chick-fil-A. These businesses invest in better recruiting. They hire happier employees and train them significantly more than anyone else in their industry. That investment also means the business will have to charge more for its services and products. So in reality, the customers pay more for smiling faces. But don't be mistaken—this is one of the greatest investments a business can make.

According to a *QSR* Magazine annual report, Chick-fil-A is the most polite chain in the restaurant business. Of the chains surveyed, that company's employees were most likely to say "please" and "thank you," and to smile at customers. "We know our customers appreciate that we can be nice while being fast and accurate," says Mark Morai-takis, senior director of hospitality and service design. "Eye contact and smiling go a long way in the drive-thru experience."[13]

It is certainly not the pay. According to Glassdoor, Chick-fil-A's pay is in line with the industry average. So why is Chick-fil-A consistently the highest-rated chain in customer satisfaction? Because the company invests more than other companies to train its employees and help them advance their careers, regardless of whether those careers are in fast food.[14]

Does this obsession with the customer experience and fanatical attention to detail really pay off? Evidently so. Along with its top ranking in restaurant customer service surveys, Chick-fil-A has generated more revenue per restaurant in recent years than any other fast-food chain in the United States. The chain's average sales per restaurant reached nearly $4 million, compared to the average KFC, which sold $1 million. Customer service is the key to Chick-fil-A's success, driving higher sales per unit and contributing to the chain's ability to generate higher annual sales than KFC, Pizza Hut, and Domino's, even though each of those has more than twice as many US locations.[15]

## Do You Have Employees Who Suffer from RBF?

If employee smiles generate profits, employees with RBF can have the opposite effect. For those unfamiliar with the expression, RBF stands for "resting bitch face" and refers to an expression that is perceived as angry, irritated, or blank, even when the person is at ease. It may be caused subconsciously or when an employee is focused on a job, but the result is that the person seems unapproachable. RBF, once considered a parody or a joke, is now being taken more seriously. Plastic surgeons say they are fielding a growing number of requests from those who want to surgically correct their "permafrowns." David B. Givens, director of the Center for Nonverbal Studies in Spokane, Washington, calls the condition "blank face" and points out that people judge a neutral, expressionless face to be "unfriendly."[16]

> No matter what you call it, displaying RBF gives customers a perception of what your mood is. As science has long proved, people make judgments based on facial cues . . . people who look "happy" are generally deemed more trustworthy and approachable as well.

I am not a fan of the term RBF because the word "bitch" is sexist, and plenty of men also suffer from RBF. We have heard the condition labeled GF, for "grumpy face," or CF, for "constipated face." You can coin your own phrase.

No matter what you call it, displaying RBF gives customers a perception of your mood. As science has long proved, people make judgments based on facial cues. Studies have found that people are less likely to find friendly-looking faces guilty of crimes; people who look "happy" are generally deemed more trustworthy and approachable as well.[17]

RBF is something to be taken seriously in any business with customer-facing and customer-interacting employees, whether the interaction is face-to-face, ear-to-ear, or click-to-click. A smile is just as much a part of a uniform as anything else employees are required to wear. Consider it part of a dress code—uniform, name tag, tie, and a smile. In my companies, we have sent team members home for being "out of uniform," for not smiling. Everyone should have a smile, and it should be genuine. I like to tell my employees, "If you are happy, tell your face."

# How to Determine Who Has RBF in Your Company

Many times good, happy employees are guilty of RBF, but they are just not aware of their "crime." To remedy that, I have had my employees photographed in action, when interacting with a customer both face-to-face and while on the phone. I was shocked at the wide variety of facial expressions I saw. One thing was consistent, though; the team members who had smiles always had smiles, the ones who didn't have smiles usually never had them.

Many of the employees who rarely smiled when with customers are just as nice, if not nicer, than the smiling employees. However, that was not necessarily the perception of the customer or coworker. When I showed my employees their RBF photos, they were horrified. They had no idea that is how they looked when they were dealing with customers, and they all were determined to change. I love how author Jeffrey Gitomer says it: "Lead with a smile and earn a smile from everyone you talk to."

# Talk Less, Smile More

Quoting a line from the play *Hamilton*, "Talk less, smile more," billionaire Richard Branson adds, "If everyone did this the world would be a happier place. Stopping to really listen, pay attention to your companion, and truly hear what they are saying, is all too rare. Often we are too quick to step in and talk over them, especially in the business world. When you take a step back, smile, and listen, it can be really rewarding. It will also often end up in a more meaningful connection, which will in turn lead to more smiles."[18]

Smiling is a necessary first step. But it's only a first step. Let's then go on to teach what kindness looks like—in business, in family, in communities, and in schools. Without the hidden agenda of making a sale or profit, businesses need to ensure that employees know how to care for others. Teach them how to display genuine interest. The fact is: If you focus on building a relationship instead of a sale, you will end up with *more* sales. A sale is something that happens while you are immersed in serving others. And the effects will be widespread. Building rapport will not only have an incredible impact on employees and customers but also on your personal life.

> *"Serving others is the meaning of why we are alive, not what we do when it is convenient or can come back to benefit ourselves."*

## CHAPTER 3 TAKEAWAYS

- Technological innovations have caused tremendous dislocations in today's workplace.

- The most memorable customer experiences are the ones where an emotional connection was made, where both customer and employee felt something.

- Customers do not want their lives filled with endless robotic encounters. As automated transactions become faster, easier, and more reliable, making the human connection will become increasingly rare—and therefore increasingly more valuable.

- Because of the digital revolution, many members of the younger generations lack the necessary people skills of previous generations. Yet they are now leading start-ups that have developed quickly into leading companies.

- These seven traits are key to effective interactions:
  - Compassion and Empathy
  - Engagement and Warmth
  - A Drive to Serve
  - Ownership
  - Charitable Assumption
  - Presence
  - The Desire to Exceed Expectations

- The ability to convince others that your ideas matter is the single greatest skill that will give you a competitive edge at a time when all professions are under attack from being automated or commoditized.

# THE TOUCH-SCREEN AGE

> *"Don't forget the 'social' part of social media."*
> —UNKNOWN

Today we are all living in the "Touch-Screen Age." This includes baby boomers as well as millennials, for although many think of the younger generation as being the most tech savvy, virtually no one has been left out. Members of every age group now use smartphones, social media, iPads, and computers. These devices are necessary parts of our lives, and although they make many things easier or more useful, when they are overused, they can negatively impact human interaction and, more importantly, our emotional state.

One result of the Touch-Screen Age is that we have significantly fewer face-to-face interactions, and when we lack those interactions, our people skills begin to erode.

As Dr. Manfred Spitzer noted in

> These devices are necessary parts of our lives, and although they make many things easier or more useful, when they are overused, they can negatively impact human interaction and, more importantly, our emotional state.

his book *Digital Dementia: What We and Our Children Are Doing to Our Minds*, "When you use the computer, you outsource your mental activity. The more time you spend with screen media, the less your social skills will be."[1]

## "Connect" and "Connection" Are Not the Same Thing

It is ironic that "social media" dramatically increases "social isolation" due to a lack of real contact and connectedness with other people. This is strongest among younger people who use technology the most. "That's because people crave human connection but nonetheless find it easier and simpler to turn to a device than to have a normal conversation," says Dan Schawbel in his book *Back to Human*. "As a result, people feel they are getting their dose of social interaction. But in reality, they are missing out on forming real relationships, which is causing isolation and depression."[2]

Nothing will ever replace looking directly into someone else's eyes and making a genuine connection. "Connect" and "connection" are not the same thing. The number of Facebook friends we have does not equal the number of relationships we have built. Social capital cannot be measured in likes and shares. While technology is constantly changing and improving to help us stay in touch with others, it will always be live, physical, real-time human interaction that builds trust and strong relationships and is the most mutually rewarding.

"If our increasing tendency to hide behind screens and devices instead of investing in our relationships is weakening our ability to achieve work and life satisfaction," says Schawbel, "what's the solution? Surely, it's to get back to being more human."[3]

# The Positive Impact Social Media Has Had on Customer Service

One of the best consequences of social media and the internet has been to shine a spotlight on problematic business practices, forcing many to improve their customer service and causing others to fall by the wayside.

For hundreds of years, the best form of advertising was word of mouth. Today, it is word of mouse. Social media represents a gigantic power shift. Customers no longer trust what a single person—even a trusted friend—says. They will go directly to the internet and see what *hundreds* of customers are saying about the experience your company

> Social media represents a gigantic power shift. Customers no longer trust what a single person—even a trusted friend—says. They will go directly to the internet and see what *hundreds* of customers are saying about the experience your company delivers.

delivers. Research shows 84 percent of people trust online reviews as much as a personal recommendation.[4] And when the experience is a negative one, consumers can share their displeasure with thousands of others at the click of a button.

> *You are either creating brand ambassadors, or brand terrorists doing brand assassination.*

A personal experience brought that home to me. One of my close friends called me and said his son, who had recently graduated from college, was living in a new city. He was looking for a good financial service firm to do business with. Did I know of any firms that could be of help? I immediately introduced the young man, via email, to the vice president of a financial service company. What could be better than a solid introduction to a senior VP by a family friend? Case closed . . . or maybe not.

A few days later I asked my friend how things were going with his son and the company I had referred him to. To my surprise he told me his son never followed up with the VP because he did some research online and didn't like the negative reviews this company had from past customers and employees. It is clear that referrals and word of mouth are no longer the number one marketing vehicle.

## The Customer Rebellion

Companies spend millions creating and advertising their brands, yet the customer's experience is what drives customer perception. Consumers have less patience and are more outspoken than ever before. They no longer tolerate subpar service, indifference, and unempathetic businesses. They are standing up for themselves and causing a customer rebellion.

Too many companies think the only answer is to get as many people as possible to share positive reviews. That helps but doesn't fix a problem if there is one. Remember, what your business does well— or not so well—will be broadcast to hundreds, if not thousands, of potential customers.

Those customers expect your company to be easy to contact and quick to respond. So you need to focus on making sure every person you do business with walks away with a positive experience, even if that means following up with customers who are initially unhappy. Follow up, make it right, don't be defensive, don't make excuses, and trust what your customer is telling you.

## Being the Brand Customers Love to Hate

Every year it seems like the majority of airlines vie for the honor of being selected as the "Worst Airline in the US." Air travel has been considered one of the most unpleasant experiences a person can encounter; and while our society has accepted it as the norm, it does appear that over the past few years, air rage has hit an all-time high.

The major US airlines have been subjecting passengers to lousy service for decades, and no one has been able to do anything about it. The airlines have apathetic employees who do not enjoy their jobs, have not been trained in hospitality, and are forced to hide behind a mountain of policy and endless red tape. The situation only got worse when major airlines started merging, giving the public even fewer options.

> We created a situation at our doing that we should not have done. Our employees did not have the authority to do what was right or use their common sense.

In the past, when a customer complained, it was simply their word against the gigantic corporation. But social media has changed that. For example, following the United Airlines incident in 2017, when a passenger was dragged off a plane, United initially blamed the passenger for being unruly. A video of the incident went viral, however, disproving United's account and showing the airline in the worst possible light. Finally United's CEO, Oscar Munoz, admitted in a late but laudable statement, "We created a situation at our doing that we should not have done. Our employees did not have the authority to do what was right or use their common sense."[5]

The truth is that the airline industry isn't conducting itself any worse today than it always has. The difference is that now problems are being caught on smartphone videos and distributed by social media. When clips go viral, they get on the news and create a public uproar that

> When clips go viral, they get on the news and create a public uproar that forces the businesses to be held accountable. No longer can customers be pushed around by businesses, because there is now video evidence online.

forces the businesses to be held accountable. No longer can customers be pushed around by businesses, because there is now video evidence online. And with video evidence, there is little room for the airline to bury a problem, manipulate the narrative, or turn the story into a he-said, she-said situation.

Feedback like this isn't limited to airlines, of course. Social media can have a similar effect in a huge range of customer-facing industries.

## The Social Media Impact on Our Mental Health

Positive consequences aside, the digital world we live in may be the most damaging invention to affect our mental health.

Full disclosure, I love technology. I love all my devices. I love checking what is going on in the world from sports to headline news. I'm always trying to keep my inbox empty and catch up on my social media channels. Most of the time I find it a relaxing escape. However, it is easy to get addicted to social media and overuse it. I have to work hard at using my devices in moderation, so it doesn't interfere with my being present with family, friends, and coworkers. I have had to implement rules and limitations for myself, and I have seen the negative side effects of the digital world on my children and friends. The information we have about these effects is sobering. The overuse of digital devices is reaching epidemic proportions.

For example, we're hearing about digital dementia, which is characterized as the deterioration of brain function as a result of the overuse of digital technology. This leads to unbalanced brain development, as heavy users are more likely to overdevelop their left brains, leaving their right brains underdeveloped.[6]

> Doctors . . . discovered that people who are heavy users of digital devices actually experience cognitive and memory problems similar to people who have sustained brain injuries.

Doctors from South Korea, which has one of the largest digital-using populations in the world, have discovered that people who are heavy users of digital devices actually experience cognitive and memory problems similar to people who have sustained brain injuries.[7] Let me repeat that: Heavy users of digital devices experience cognitive and memory problems similar to people who have sustained brain injuries.

## Slaves to Technology

As technology becomes a larger part of our lives, people actually use their brains significantly less than in the past, leaving many young people with underdeveloped brains and shorter attention spans. This negative impact may also occur in adults. Have you ever felt like your memory is getting worse? It may not be due to the natural aging process. Less frequent use of a muscle creates atrophy, and a brain is no exception. Jim Kwik, an expert in optimal brain performance, has said, "We are outsourcing our brains to our smart devices, we are so reliant on our smart phones that our smart phones are making us stupid."[8]

Mental stimulation addiction (MSA) is affecting millions of people who are smartphone junkies and who need to constantly be texting; checking Facebook, Twitter, LinkedIn, and Instagram; or carrying on a multitude of other social media habits. I am totally guilty of this. Whenever I have a few minutes of downtime, such as sitting in a waiting room or riding an elevator, I start scanning my smartphone inbox, text messages, and social media accounts. I then look at my favorite websites like ESPN and headline news. After I have exhausted all of those resources, I find myself going back through each one of them again, though absolutely nothing has changed. Sadly I struggle with simply sitting still, relaxing, and daydreaming. You can imagine the impact these distractions have on personal and professional productivity.

## The Creativity and Conversation Killer

Simply put, technology is killing our creativity. Downtime and a relaxed mental state are the best environments for our mind to veer off from mainstream thought patterns and venture into the unknown. Think about it. When have you gotten your best ideas? When you daydream. When are you most likely to daydream? Early mornings with your coffee on the patio, in the shower, on vacation, and at other idle times that now are few and far between because technology has gobbled them up.

> Technology is killing our creativity. Downtime and a relaxed mental state are the best environments for our mind to veer off from mainstream thought patterns and venture into the unknown.

Similarly, productive or just pleasurable conversation has been stifled by technology. It used to be that when a question arose, people kept talking as they sought an answer. The results were healthy discussions, debates, and creative storytelling. Today, however, we immediately turn to

Google for the answer, ending that particular line of questioning or thinking. Without those discussions, we've lost something valuable, notes Kate Unsworth, a leading expert in social change: "These are the conversations that really form bonds between people. You gain insight into the way someone's mind works, and it is not typically a conversation anyone has had before, so it is engaging and memorable."[9]

If you find yourself feeling uncreative and stale, you may be suffering from MSA. We need to protect our idle moments to let our minds rest, reset, be reinvigorated, rejuvenated, and daydream. You will be surprised at how stimulated and creative you will become.

## From Boredom to Brilliant Ideas

Insights always happen when your mind is at its quietest, says Manoush Zomorodi in a great TED Talk entitled "How Boredom Can Lead to Your Most Brilliant Ideas." Zomorodi explores what happens to our mind both when we get bored and if we never get bored. "I started talking to neuroscientists and cognitive psychologists, and what they told me was fascinating," she says. "Turns out that when you get bored, you ignite a network in your brain called the default mode. So our body goes on autopilot while we're folding the laundry or we're walking to work, but actually that is when our brain gets really busy. I learned that in the default mode is when we connect disparate ideas, we solve some of our most nagging problems, and we do something called autobiographical planning. This is when

Some of them told me that they didn't recognize some of the emotions that they felt during challenge week, because, if you think about it, if you have never known life without connectivity, you may never have experienced boredom.

we look back at our lives, we take note of the big moments, we create a personal narrative, and then we set goals and we figure out what steps we need to take to reach them."[10]

Zomorodi actually held a "Bored and Brilliant" challenge, calling for times in the day where you unplugged from your smartphone and social media. Her feedback from the thousands of people who accepted the challenge was incredible, especially from those in the younger generation. "Some of them told me that they didn't recognize some of the emotions that they felt during challenge week, because, if you think about it, if you have never known life without connectivity, you may never have experienced boredom," she says.[11]

"Researchers at USC studied teenagers who are on social media while they're talking to their friends or doing homework. They found that two years down the road, these teenagers were less creative and imaginative about their own personal futures and about solving societal problems, like violence in their neighborhoods. And we really need this next generation to be able to focus on some big problems: climate change, economic disparity, and massive cultural differences. No wonder CEOs in an IBM survey identified creativity as the number-one leadership competency," Zomorodi concludes.[12]

> These teenagers were less creative and imaginative about their own personal futures and about solving societal problems.

## There Ain't No App for Relationship Building

The social media world we live in has additional negative implications for our younger generations. In an interview on *Inside Quest*, organizational consultant Simon Sinek cites research by Harvard scientists that reported how social media can activate pleasure sensations in the brain similar to food, money, and sex. The dopamine highs and lows were as addictive as drinking, smoking, and gambling.[13] Sinek notes:

> *What we are seeing is as they grow older, too many kids don't know how to form deep, meaningful relationships. They will admit that many of their relationships are superficial; they will admit that they don't count on their friends; they don't rely on their friends. Deep meaningful relationships are not there because they never practiced the skillset and worse, they don't have the coping mechanisms to deal with stress. So when significant stress begins to show up in their lives, they're not turning to a person, they're turning to a device, they're turning to social media, they're turning to these things which offer temporary relief.*
>
> *Everything you want you can have instantaneously . . . instant gratification, except, job satisfaction and strength of relationships—there ain't no app for that. They are slow, meandering, uncomfortable, messy processes.*[14]

As a result, businesses that want to be successful need to address this relationship-building deficit in their employee training. Companies need to find ways to train younger staff members on things they may lack such as social skills and rapport building.

Sometimes it comes down to basic politeness. Kids who are growing up with Alexa and Siri are getting in the habit of barking out commands and getting immediate responses multiple times a day. Some people feel this is affecting youngsters' manners when

> As a result, businesses that want to be successful need to address this relationship-building deficit in their employee training. Companies need to find ways to train younger staff members on things they may lack such as social skills and rapport building.

they interact with actual humans. I personally would like to see chatbots and artificial intelligence perform requests only when "Please" and "Thank you" are used.

How bad has the technology epidemic gotten? The companies that created the problem are now trying to provide solutions to help people use these devices in moderation. Apple introduced an app called Screen Time, which allows users to monitor and limit their app usage on the iPhone and iPad. In addition to helping people curb the time spent on devices, it allows parents to remotely track and limit their children's use of those devices—a response to growing societal concern that adults and children are too focused on phones.[15]

Screen Time also has an "App Limits" feature. This allows users to set a daily time limit for a particular app or an entire category of apps (social media, productivity, entertainment, and so on). When the limit is hit, the user will be blocked from further access to that software. Downtime, which cuts off access to any apps a user wants shut down at night, is another tool to help people shift focus away from technology before bedtime.

## Time for a Digital Detox

If it seems a bit ironic to turn to technology for a solution to technology, why not just embrace a digital detox? That means switching off all electronic devices (mobiles, smartphones, tablets, laptops, and computers) for a certain length of time. One case study featured in *Fast Company*, "What Really Happens to Your Brain and Body during a Digital Detox" by Elizabeth Segran, shows that after three days without technology, people began to make better eye contact instead of looking down to their screens. This eye contact also appeared to encourage people to connect with one another more deeply. They were able to relax into conversations and seemed more empathetic toward one another.[16]

"Even after a few days without technology, people were more likely to remember obscure details about one another, such as the names of distant relatives mentioned in passing," says Segran. "The neuroscientists believe that this is because people were more present in conversation, so their brains were able to process and store new information more easily. With the many distractions of technology, our brains have been trained not to register seemingly insignificant details, which is very important in the process of bonding and learning about other people."[17]

Segran also found this surprising consequence: "One of the most powerful findings was that people tended to make significant changes to their lives when they were offline for a while. Some decided to make big changes in their career or relationships. The lack of constant distraction appeared to free people's minds to contemplate more important issues in their lives, and it also made them believe they had the willpower to sustain a transformation."[18]

> The lack of constant distraction appeared to free people's minds to contemplate more important issues in their lives, and it also made them believe they had the willpower to sustain a transformation.

## Technology Time Out

If you're not ready to completely cut off all digital devices, consider a more gradual approach. At home, try not using technology for the first 30-45 minutes after you wake and during the last two hours before you retire for the evening. Banning technology at the dinner table and when out to dinner is an obvious step, but you can also prohibit your family from using devices during car rides of 20 minutes or less. One of my personal favorite remedies is to try exercising without listening or watching anything; just let your mind wander. I warn you, you will need a notepad as soon as you are done because of all the ideas that will come to you.

Would you love your employees to have more creative conversations? Consider holding company meetings where everyone, from senior leadership to frontline associates, leaves all technology outside the room. This includes smartphones, laptops, tablets, and smart watches. When employees ask, "What will I use to take notes?" introduce them to notepads and pens.

## It Is Time to Build a Relationship with Yourself

Actions like these are not about giving up all social media or devices completely; they are about finding a balance. There is an incredible YouTube video titled *Look Up*, with more than 60 million views, that cleverly emphasizes the importance of making sure you are awake, alive, and living life in the moment, instead of living your life through a screen. The following are a few of *Look Up*'s important insights.[19]

> *I have 422 friends, yet I am lonely . . . I looked around, and then realized that this media we call social, is anything but. When we open our computers, and it's our doors we shut . . . All this technology we have, it's just an illusion, of community, companionship, a sense of inclusion, yet when you step away from this device of delusion, you awaken to see a world of confusion . . . It's not very*

*likely you will make world's greatest dad, if you can't entertain a child without using an iPad . . . So look up from your phone, shut down that display, take in your surroundings, and make the most of today. Just one real connection is all it can take, to show you the difference that being there can make . . . Don't give in to a life where you follow the hype, give people your love, don't give them your like. Disconnect from the need to be heard and defined. Go out into the world; leave distractions behind. Look up from your phone, shut down that display, stop watching this video, live life the real way.*[20]

## CHAPTER 4 TAKEAWAYS

- Today every generation is living in the Touch-Screen Age.

- These devices are necessary parts of our lives, and although they make many things easier or more useful, when they are over-used, they can negatively impact human interaction and, more importantly, our emotional state.

- Social media dramatically increases social isolation.

- Social media represents a gigantic power shift. Customers go directly to the internet and see what hundreds of customers are saying about the experience your company delivers.

- When clips go viral, they get on the news and create a public uproar that forces the businesses to be held accountable. No longer can customers be pushed around by businesses.

- Doctors discovered that people who are heavy users of digital devices actually experience cognitive and memory problems similar to people who have sustained brain injuries.

- Mental stimulation addiction (MSA) is affecting millions of people who are technology junkies and who need to constantly be stimulated by their devices.

- Technology is killing our creativity. Downtime and a relaxed mental state are the best environments for our mind to veer off from mainstream thought patterns and venture into the unknown.

- A study done on teenagers who were heavy users of social media showed that two years down the road they were less creative and imaginative about their own personal futures and about solving societal problems.

- CEOs surveyed identified creativity as the number one leadership competency.

- Businesses that want to be successful need to address this relationship-building deficit in their employee training. Companies need to find ways to train younger staff members who may have missed out on honing social skills and building rapport with others.

- It is time to build a relationship with yourself.

# MEET AS STRANGERS, LEAVE AS FRIENDS

> *"Act as if today is the day you will be remembered for how you treat others."*

Despite all the advances in technology and the presence of social media in our world, the single biggest factor contributing to where you are today remains the relationships you have acquired over your lifetime. The people in your life have significantly impacted your professional and personal success, happiness, and accomplishments. They are the ones who have influenced you, inspired you, taught you, believed in you, and stood by you. That will be true 10 and 20 years from now. It will be true when you are on your deathbed reflecting on the life you have lived.

It is human nature to be preoccupied with what is happening in our world. However, in order to build a connection with another person, we need to put our

> The single biggest factor contributing to where you are today remains the relationships you have acquired over your lifetime.

focus on *them*, particularly on making that person feel better for having interacted with us. When we are totally present with someone, that's when the magic happens. Above all, this depends on forgoing a desire to focus on ourselves and our own story.

I couldn't agree more with the following statement by Stephen Covey:

> *People don't listen with the intent of understanding; they listen with the intent of replying.*

Scientists have studied the human brain and found it takes a minimum of 0.6 seconds to formulate a response to something said. Then they researched hundreds of conversations and found the average gap between people talking was 0.2 seconds. How is it that people can respond in 1/3 the time that the human brain allows? Obviously people have their responses ready long before the other person has finished talking.[1]

> **Scientists have studied the human brain and found it takes a minimum of 0.6 seconds to formulate a response to something said. Then they researched hundreds of conversations and found the average gap between people talking was 0.2 seconds.**

We have to change that habit. The great Jim Rohn, an entrepreneur and motivational speaker, once said, "The greatest gift you can give someone is the gift of your attention."

How does this translate to our professional life? In business we need to focus on collecting customer intelligence. This doesn't mean how smart our customers are, but rather how smart we are about our customers. Customer intelligence is customer data (for example, personal information, purchasing history, referrals, personal preferences, home address, and workplace) that fuels rapport building.

I love asking audiences, "How many people feel that you are pretty good at building rapport with others?" A majority of hands always go up. Then I tell them, "I don't believe you; just because you had a conversation with someone for the last 15–20 minutes doesn't mean you built a rapport. You might have been talking about yourself the entire time."

## Made a Connection with Someone? Prove It

In order to prove that you made a connection with someone after a conversation you need to walk away knowing two or more facts about their FORD.

That stands for:

- Family

- Occupation

- Recreation

- Dreams

If you can find out about two of these subjects, you not only have a relationship, you *own* that relationship. FORD represents people's hot buttons, what each individual cares about the most. FORD is what they are passionate about. It is the topics that make them light up, that they

FORD represents people's hot buttons, what each individual cares about the most. FORD is what they are passionate about. It is the topics that make them light up. Constantly referring to FORD keeps the focus of the conversation on the other person.

talk about in detail. Constantly referring to FORD keeps the focus of the conversation on the other person. Here are some examples of the type of information you can casually collect about FORD.

## FAMILY

For most people, this is the hottest button of all. Are they married? How long have they been married? Do they have kids? How old are their kids? What activities are their kids into? Where was their most recent family trip?

## OCCUPATION

What do they do for a living? What is their title? How long have they worked at their current job? What was their degree in? How did they get into this industry?

## RECREATION

What are their hobbies? What do they do for fun, with their free time? What do they do for exercise—running, lifting, yoga, and so on? Do they have a favorite team, sport, college?

## DREAMS

What are their long-term goals? Where are they dying to travel? What is on their bucket list?

Every time you communicate with a customer, regardless if it is over the phone, electronically, or face-to-face, you should be collecting and utilizing customer intelligence. That doesn't mean you interrogate them; you are not rattling off question after question to tick off the answers to each item of their FORD. However, it's extremely simple to work in a few questions about these subjects in the natural flow of a conversation. I have been intentionally practicing the FORD technique in every conversation for more than a decade, and no one has ever said to me, "You sure ask a lot of questions." It is quite the opposite. Once you get someone talking, typically they will end up offering most of the information all on their own. All you have to do is sit back and listen.

Everyone you come in contact with has an invisible sign above his or her head that reads:

*"Make Me Feel Important!"*

## Collecting Customer Intelligence

The best way to make this a part of your daily habits is to create a system for collecting and retrieving people's FORD, whether on a notepad, in your contacts app on your mobile phone, or in the customer relationship management (CRM) software on your computer.

These tools help us focus on all the customer intelligence thrown at us each day. For instance, customer

The best way to make this a part of your daily habits is to create a system for collecting and retrieving people's FORD, whether on a notepad, in your contacts app on your mobile phone, or in the customer relationship management (CRM) software on your computer.

intelligence notepads are ideal for professionals on the run, in meetings, and at networking events. As soon as you walk away from the customer, prospect, neighbor, or person you just met, write down the key things they just told you (for example, leaving for a vacation, alumnus of Northwestern University, has a daughter on a traveling volleyball team).

Personally, there are four things I always make sure I have with me when I leave the house: my wallet, car keys, cell phone, and customer intelligence notepad. I never leave home without the notepad. It reminds me to focus on the other person's FORD in my daily interactions.

FORD desk pads are useful when you are at your desk communicating over the phone and electronically. Use them immediately; then, when you have a moment later in the day, you can enter the information into your CRM system for retrieval the next time you are communicating with that person.

Many of our clients who have contact/call centers use FORD desk pads. That doesn't mean we want customer service representatives asking a customer about their FORD when someone is scheduling an appointment. That would be like creating a stalker checklist. But, as most of you know, you don't need to ask those kinds of questions; people tend to over-share. They will say, "I need to reschedule my 3 p.m. appointment on Wednesday because my daughter's high school soccer team just made it to district." If we quickly respond, "Okay, how about Thursday at 4?" we completely miss the excellent FORD offered by the customer. If you capture the FORD, however, when the customer comes in on Thursday, the receptionist can greet her with, "How did your daughter's soccer team do at districts?" The customer, forgetting that she ever mentioned it, responds, "They won, how did you know?"

## Priming the Mind

Did you ever buy a new car model in a color you were sure you had never seen before? Yet an hour later, you notice several of the same model and color on the road. Did a bunch of people have the same idea as you that day and purchase that same car in the same hue? No! Your mind has been primed to see what has always been there. Using FORD tools when communicating with others is an excellent way to prime your mind to notice and hear information you otherwise would have missed.

> Using FORD tools when communicating with others is an excellent way to prime your mind to notice and hear information you otherwise would have missed.

After my oldest son, Johnni, went off to college, he called me and said, "Dad, FORD is the best thing ever." I was stunned; he had never listened to anything I had ever told him before. He then went on to say, "It is an amazing way to meet girls on campus." Glad I was able to help.

Collecting customer intelligence is meant to enhance your listening and awareness skills, not to hamper your productivity. The DiJulius Group worked with a consulting client who hired us to work with its customer service department, which handles inside sales and support for clients. Part of revamping its customer experience was introducing them to the importance of collecting FORD and rolling out customer intelligence desk pads. We told their representatives not to do anything different on the call with their clients. We did not want them to ask any questions that were on the customer intelligence pads (for example, about their FORD). Given the amount of calls they handled per day, we didn't want to make them less productive but rather more effective at making personal connections.

All we asked them to do was write down anything on their customer intelligence pads that their customers voluntarily shared regarding FORD. Within the first week, one of the customer service reps went into her supervisor's office and said basically, "I know Jim, from ABC Company, was a secret shopper for you today to see if I would record any of his customer intelligence. He told me more today than he has told me in the five years we have been having a weekly call." Her boss responded, "I have not spoken to Jim or to any of your customers."

The fact is, the customer service rep heard more that day than she had ever heard before because she was listening. For instance, when she said, "Okay, Jim, I will talk to you next Wednesday," Jim responded with "No, that won't work. My family and I will be on vacation in Orlando all next week. It will have to be in two weeks." Bam! She heard it, she caught that, and instead of going into transactional processing mode, she was now able to capitalize on Jim's FORD. She could do one of several things: tell him to have a great vacation; follow up with him in two weeks and ask him about his vacation to Orlando; or maybe, if he was a VIP customer, she might say, "Orlando, that is great. Where are you staying?" Then she could make sure to have some surprise (such as a fruit tray or bottle of wine) waiting in his hotel room upon his arrival in Orlando.

> The critical piece is that you create a system that helps you pay more attention to hearing and obtaining your customer's information so you can document it and follow up, demonstrating that you are not like anyone else with whom they do business.

It doesn't matter how you collect customer intelligence. The critical piece is that you create a system that helps you pay more attention to hearing and obtaining your customer's information so you can document it and follow up, demonstrating that you are not like anyone else with whom they do business. You show that you genuinely care about them as a person who has a life, and not just the next customer you are handling, processing, selling to, or supporting.

## The Art of Listening

"Listening to understand is often the only way of showing people they are special and that you care for them," says Rich Simmonds in his blog, *The Art of Listening*. He adds, "If you are unable to connect with people to the point that they can trust you, they will not follow you as a leader or give you the opportunity to serve them as a leader (or as a salesperson, for that matter). These are the basics of a relationship, and trust will only be sustainable in the safety of a relationship.[2]

"If we don't listen to understand, we will never hear what the insecurities of others are, and we will probably never understand our own insecurities either. Yes, we all have insecurities. It is our task to show people we care, not so that we can blatantly manipulate them into using our product or service, but rather by listening and trying to understand them where they are," Simmons also points out. "This is listening with empathy and we will understand what their insecurities are, what their real needs are and we will be able to tailor solutions that suit them so that a win/win situation arises for everybody."[3]

How can you perfect the art of listening? Ask fascinating, probing questions, follow-up questions, and then even more questions. Then be silent and let the person speak their piece. You learn valuable insights not from asking one question, but through an unstructured back-and-forth dialogue. As Tom Peters notes in his book *The Excellence Dividend,* "If you ask a question and don't ask two or three follow-up questions, odds are you weren't listening to the answer. A good listener becomes INVISIBLE; makes the respondent the centerpiece."[4]

Peters dedicates an entire chapter to listening. He writes, "Attention is one thing. FIERCE attention resides on a different planet. Fierce attention is a degree of attentiveness that is palpable, that makes you (the one responding to the comment or question) feel fully engaged and at the center of the universe. The point is not to listen or even to get better at listening. The point is to unabashedly make listening (fierce listening) the centerpiece of your existence—to make it no less than your strategic strength/strategic differentiator number one."[5]

> If you ask a question and don't ask two or three follow-up questions, odds are you weren't listening to the answer. A good listener becomes INVISIBLE; makes the respondent the centerpiece.

It is not about listening to decide when to chime in with your own opinion; it is about listening to actually understand. Asking these two questions can dramatically help anyone's ability to listen to understand: "Tell me more" and "Help me understand."

> *"The best way to persuade someone is with your ears, by listening to them."*
> —FORMER US SECRETARY OF STATE DEAN RUSK[6]

## Myths of a Good Listener

In their *Harvard Business Review* article, "What Great Listeners Actually Do," authors Jack Zenger and Joseph Folkman found that most people believe they are better-than-average listeners. They share the myth that people believe good listening comes down to:

1.  Not talking when others are speaking

2.  Letting others know you're listening through facial expressions and verbal sounds ("*mmm-hmm*")

3.  Being able to repeat word for word what others have said. We have all been taught this practice and heard the following comment: "So, let me make sure I understand you. What you're saying is . . . "[7]

Research suggests that these behaviors fall far short of superior listening skills. The article cites a study comparing the best listeners to average listeners and identifying the characteristics that make an outstanding listener:

- **Good listening is much more than being silent.** It is actually the opposite; people perceive the best listeners to be those who periodically ask questions that stimulate further discovery and insight. Sitting silently nodding does not provide sure evidence that a person is listening. Good listening was consistently seen as a two-way dialog. The best conversations were active.

- **"Good listening included interactions that build a person's self-esteem.** The best listeners made the conversation a positive experience for the other party, which doesn't happen when the listener is passive. Good listeners made the other person feel supported and conveyed confidence in them."

- **"Good listening was seen as a cooperative conversation.** In these interactions, feedback flowed smoothly in both directions with neither party becoming defensive about comments the other made. By contrast, poor listeners were seen as competitive—as listening only to identify errors in reasoning or logic, using their silence as a chance to prepare their next response. That might make you an excellent debater, but it doesn't make you a good listener. Good listeners may challenge assumptions and disagree, but the person being listened to feels the listener is trying to help, not wanting to win an argument."

- **"Good listeners tended to make suggestions.** Good listening invariably included some feedback provided in a way others would accept and that opened up alternative paths to consider."[8]

This was my favorite part of the HBR article: "While many of us have thought of being a good listener being like a sponge that accurately absorbs what the other person is saying, instead, what these findings show is that good listeners are like trampolines. They are someone you can bounce ideas off of—and rather than absorbing your ideas and energy, they amplify, energize, and clarify your thinking. They make you feel better not merely passively absorbing, but by

> These findings show that good listeners are like trampolines. They are someone you can bounce ideas off of—and rather than absorbing your ideas and energy, they amplify, energize, and clarify your thinking.

actively supporting. This lets you gain energy and height, just like someone jumping on a trampoline."[9]

## The Conversation Is the Relationship

When you are able to show genuine interest in someone, with the goal of building a relationship, instead of trying to get something out of him or her, the friendship ends up being the greatest reward.

In her book *Fierce Conversations*, Susan Scott makes this point extremely well: "Our most valuable currency is relationships . . . In every conversation, meeting, or e-mail we are accumulating or losing emotional capital, building relationships we enjoy or endure with colleagues, bosses, customers, and vendors." Scott also notes that in order to be a great communicator, you need to have a totally open mind in every conversation you have. She says, "People don't cling to their positions as the undeniable truth. Instead, they consider their views as hypotheses to be explored and tested against others."[10]

> When you are able to show genuine interest in someone, with the goal of building a relationship, instead of trying to get something out of him or her, the friendship ends up being the greatest reward.

## You Can't Be Listening If You Are Talking

Jerome Groopman, a physician and Harvard medical school professor, wrote *How Doctors Think*. He asserts that the key to collecting useful information and solving the patient's health puzzle is to let the patient say her or his piece. However, Groopman cites research that demonstrates doctors repeatedly interrupt the patient presenting their symptoms after just *18 seconds*. Why? Because the average doctor (or consultant, lawyer, accountant, or financial advisor) feels he knows what the patient/client is going to say and is ready to give a professional recommendation before allowing the patient to finish explaining their problem.[11]

> Research demonstrates doctors repeatedly interrupt the patient presenting their symptoms after just 18 seconds. Why? Because the average doctor (or consultant, lawyer, accountant, or financial advisor) feels he knows what the patient/client is going to say and is ready to give a professional recommendation before allowing the patient to finish explaining their problem.

Hijacking someone's story or stepping on their message is a horrible habit that demonstrates a conversation is more about us than the person we are communicating with. Often we do this by completing the other person's thought. While we may think we are demonstrating that we are paying attention, the practice is rude; we are not allowing the other person to feel completely heard.

The highest form of respect we can show another person is genuinely listening and giving them our undivided attention. However, the listener also benefits dramatically, because it is only when we are listening that we learn, that new ideas arise, and that solutions are realized. Listening needs to be something we practice daily. There may be no better ROI.

---

*"Never miss a good chance to shut up."*
—WILL ROGERS[12]

## Do Not Be Quick to Share Your Accolades

Being a detective is a fun way to get to know people and keep the conversation focused on them. It is just as important to allow the person you're conversing with to have to spend some time finding out in-depth information on you. Think about movies: The plot is not revealed at the beginning. That would ruin the suspense. Especially do not volunteer information about yourself that can appear boastful or arrogant, though that is easier said than done.

I know this firsthand, since, unfortunately, I have been guilty of doing something similar. One incident really stands out—and hopefully it will be the last time I do this. Recently I was having dinner with my significant other, Claudia. We were dining at the bar at a restaurant, which is always our favorite way to eat out. Sitting close together makes it easier to have an intimate conversation, and I feel you always get better service at a bar since the bartender is always in sight. As we usually do, we started chatting with the customer next to us. After a while we introduced ourselves. When I said my name, he said, "Didn't you write a book?" And I responded, "I have written four." At that point I felt like an ass, and the look on Claudia's face confirmed it. It was a painful lesson.

## Conversation Nevers

- Never multitask.

- Never ask a question because you are dying to answer it yourself.

- Never ask a question and hijack someone's answer.

- Never finish the other person's sentences. (I struggle with this one because sometimes people take a long time to get to a point. To help speed it up, I will finish their sentence, which is extremely impolite.)

- Never steal someone's thunder. Suspend your own ego and let them enjoy their own story. (This is a tough one for many because when someone brings up something that you have in common, you can get excited to share your experience. For instance, you might ask someone where he or she went for spring break. Perhaps they respond excitedly, "We went to Disney World for the first time!" The listener might then respond innocently, "I love Disney. We have been there several times." But this can steal the other person's moment or make them feel like they are being one-upped.)

- Never volunteer information about yourself that appears to be bragging.

## Conversation Always

- Always remove any distractions (digital devices, for example), demonstrating your full attention on the other person.

- Always listen with your eyes. Make eye contact the entire time.

- Always be an active listener. Ask interesting and probing questions, follow-up questions, and then more questions. Then be silent and let the person speak their piece.

- Always show empathy and support in a nonjudgmental way.

- Always be patient. Let the other person speak their piece, finish their thought, feel heard.

- Always wait two seconds to process what you heard before responding.

- Always be in learning mode; everyone has something to teach.

- Always make the person speaking the focus of your attention.

- Always collect FORD (family, occupation, recreation, and dreams) and document the intelligence for future use.

- Always commit to a follow-up (when it is called for) or action plan in a specific amount of time.

One of my biggest pet peeves as a business owner is when I meet a customer who cannot remember whom she dealt with in one of my businesses. I tell my employees that this is the worst insult you can receive. Your presence and experience were so unmemorable that the customer can't even remember your name? Ara Bagdasarian, former vice president of TravelCenters of America and one of our clients, said it best, "We better know our customers' names, but if you really delivered a great experience, the customer remembers *our* name."

> *"It is not your client and prospect's job to remember you. It is your responsibility to make sure they do not have the chance to forget you."*
> —PATRICIA FRIPP

## Insatiable Curiosity

The best relationship builders appear like detectives in their conversations, looking for clues to finding out what makes the other person unique and memorable. They're after things you won't find on their Facebook page or LinkedIn profile. "Highly empathic people have an insatiable curiosity about strangers," said Roman Krznaric, author of

*Empathy: Why It Matters, and How to Get It.* "They will talk to the person sitting next to them on the bus. Curiosity expands our empathy when we talk to people outside our usual social circle, encountering lives and worldviews very different from our own."[13]

The authors of the book *Superconnector* explain how great connectors operate: "Connectors have small talk with a purpose. They are never just engaging in conversation for the sake of conversation. They always have a clear goal in mind: to extract the most pointed and relevant information about the other person. Connectors don't have casual conversations just to kill time. They are probing for a reason—to see what this person is all about, to create context for a profile that they can use later."[14]

> Highly empathic people have an insatiable curiosity about strangers. They will talk to the person sitting next to them on the bus.

## The Likability Factor

Some people are "connectors" by nature. I have long marveled at how easily my brother in-law Eddie Cheyfitz connects with total strangers and builds amazing relationships. He is one of the most liked people I have ever met. He and my sister Kathy met and started dating in the eighth grade. They just celebrated their 44th wedding anniversary, and they still have an amazing relationship. You will rarely see one without the other. Their life hasn't always been easy, however. They have overcome two major obstacles. For one thing, Kathy had their first child, a baby boy named Andy, during their senior year in high school. Eighteen years later, Andy was killed in a tragic automobile accident. Both those kinds of events often lead to divorce, so for this couple to have maintained an amazing relationship is incredible.

But there's more to the story. Because he became a father in high school, Eddie was unable to go to college. He spent 10 years working full-time at a grocery store, until one day, out of the blue, the grocery store closed down. That ended up being the best thing that ever happened to Eddie. It forced him to explore new career opportunities. To pay the bills, he started working in construction, then stumbled on a temporary part-time summer job as an ice cream merchandiser for Carnation—part of the Nestlé corporation—to help introduce a new line of ice cream novelties to grocery stores in northeast Ohio. Eddie gave up a $20-an-hour construction job for a temporary $6-an-hour position in the hope it would lead to a long-term opportunity. Not surprisingly, because of the customer relationships Eddie built in a short amount of time, his sales outperformed many others. As a result, Carnation offered him a full-time, entry-level position. Once Eddie got his foot in the door, his career took off, and he enjoyed a successful 28-year tenure at Nestlé.

Around the time Eddie was retiring, I started a nonprofit called Believe in Dreams, which fulfills the dreams of economically disadvantaged youth who have survived nonmedical adversity by providing access to enriching opportunities, connections to community, and hope for the future. I needed someone to run Believe in Dreams full-time, and I was able to talk Eddie into doing that. I couldn't have asked for a better person. He was superb at engaging people—from our dreamers (young children), volunteers, and the counselors who nominate their students to big donors who help financially support the charity. As a result of Eddie's efforts, Believe in Dreams has really taken off and has impacted many children's lives.

## Breaking the Ice

So what is Eddie's secret? How does he so easily connect with people and build amazing relationships? I have seen him do it hundreds of times: He will meet someone and within a few minutes have this total stranger sharing amazing details about him- or herself. First of all, Eddie possesses the five characteristics needed to master rapport building that we noted in chapter 1: He is authentic; he is genuinely curious; he is a great listener; he displays incredible empathy; and he absolutely loves people.

Eddie points to the questions he asks when he meets someone as his ability to build instant rapport with others. He says, "Over the years, I developed a routine that I would use in my sales calls that was a good ice breaker, asking, 'Where are you going? Where have you been?' to give me an opportunity to learn more about my customers on a personal level. People love to talk about past and future vacations."

> Over the years, I developed a routine that I would use in my sales calls that would be a good ice breaker, asking, "Where are you going? Where have you been?" to give me an opportunity to learn more about my customers on a personal level. People love to talk about past and future vacations.

Eddie continues, "It puts them in a happy place where they can share personal stories and make suggestions on great places they've been to. I also love to share vacation stories and places I have been. I found that many customers would call me when planning a trip and ask me for advice on places to visit. I always opened our dialogue about personal fun stuff. When it got time to discuss business, my job was a lot easier."

## Our Superpowers for Understanding Others

We spend much of our time trying to understand what our customers, employees, significant others, and children really mean by what they say or don't say. Too often we try to analyze, decode, or judge without ever knowing what is going on.

"Empathy is a real-life human super power," says Dr. Ali Hill, sociologist and emotional intelligence evangelist. "When we truly empathize with others, we come as close to reading minds as humans can get. When we turn off our analysis mechanisms and instead just listen and attempt to think from the other person's point of view, the message becomes much clearer. When we empathize, we

> When we truly empathize with others, we come as close to reading minds as humans can get. When we turn off our analysis mechanisms and instead just listen and attempt to think from the other person's point of view, the message becomes much clearer.

can actually feel what the other person is feeling. And when we can feel what someone else feels, then we inherently understand what they're trying to communicate. Pretty powerful stuff, empathy."[15]

Empathy is especially effective when paired with compassion. Compassion is the desire to help another person. Together empathy and compassion are the two most powerful soft skills employees can have. When you genuinely serve with compassion and empathy, your customer service rises to a completely different level. The challenge for most companies is how to teach these skills. How do you make them more than just buzzwords and platitudes? The answer is by having your employees

> When your employees really understand the customer's plight, what they're going through, the importance of each and every interaction becomes crystal clear.

constantly putting themselves in the shoes of the customer. When your employees really understand the customer's plight, what they're going through, the importance of each and every interaction becomes crystal clear.

The ability to see things from the perspective of others is key to making a connection, building a relationship, and achieving overall business success. It allows you to explore other people's viewpoints and the possibility that your opinion may be wrong.

I have admired people who always try to see things from the other person's side, even when the other person appears to be completely in the wrong. For instance, let's say you have just encountered a negative person being rude, someone we would call a jerk. Yet your friend says, "See it from their side . . . if you were in their shoes, you might feel and react the same way." Having empathy, experts say, improves your leadership, teaches you to ask the right questions, boosts teamwork, and allows you to understand your customers.[16] It is a powerful gift.

Forging strong relationships relies on all these skills—being interested in someone else's life, truly listening, and practicing empathy and compassion. They're the building blocks of the Relationship Economy.

> "Don't concentrate on making a lot of money, but rather on becoming the type of person people want to do business with."
> —ARTHUR HENRY FRIPP

**CHAPTER 5 TAKEAWAYS**

- The single biggest factor contributing to where you are today remains the relationships you have acquired over your lifetime.

- It is human nature to be preoccupied with what is happening in our world. However, in order to build a connection with another person, we need to put our focus on *them*, particularly on making that person feel better for having interacted with us.

- Scientists have studied the human brain and found it takes a minimum of 0.6 seconds to formulate a response to something said. Then they researched hundreds of conversations and found the average gap between people talking was 0.2 seconds. The greatest gift you can give someone is the gift of your attention.

- In order to prove that you made a connection with someone after a conversation you need to walk away knowing two or more facts about their FORD: family, occupation, recreation, and dreams.

- FORD represents people's hot buttons, what each individual cares about the most. FORD is what people are passionate about. It is the topics that make them light up. Constantly referring to FORD keeps the focus of the conversation on the other person.

- Using FORD tools when communicating with others is an excellent way to prime your mind to notice and hear information you otherwise would have missed.

- If you ask a question and don't ask two or three follow-up questions, odds are you weren't listening to the answer. A good listener becomes invisible and makes the respondent the centerpiece.

- Research demonstrates professionals repeatedly interrupt their customers after just *18 seconds*. Why? Because they feel they know what the customer is going to say and are ready to give a professional recommendation before allowing the customer to finish explaining their problem.

- Highly empathic people have an insatiable curiosity about strangers. They will talk to the person sitting next to them on the bus.

- When we truly empathize with others, we come as close to reading minds as humans can get. When we turn off our analysis mechanisms and instead just listen and attempt to think from the other person's point of view, the message becomes much clearer.

- When your employees really understand the customer's plight, what they're going through, the importance of each and every interaction becomes crystal clear.

# THE RELATIONSHIP ECONOMY
# IN ACTION

> *"Customer experience should be measured by one thing:*
> *how you made the customer feel."*

A s I've pointed out in previous chapters, relationships are the foundation of virtually everything that happens in our life. The quality and depth of the relationships we build determine the ability to obtain our goals and success in life. In business, effective professional relationships are critical to the daily performance of leaders, employees, and the company as a whole.

Measurements of performance such as sales, customer retention, operational productivity, cross-functional collaboration, employee retention, and leadership development all depend on healthy, productive relationships between people. So how

So how do companies and their leaders know where they stand on their most important business relationships? By making reliable, effective systems that enable employees to consistently work at the development of their relationships and assess their progress.

do companies and their leaders know where they stand on their most important business relationships? By making reliable, effective systems that enable employees to consistently work at the development of their relationships and assess their progress. This chapter probes the ways many companies accomplish that.

## Your Relationship Report Card

To demonstrate how critical and dependent we are on others, The DiJulius Group uses the following exercise called Your Relationship Report Card. There are three parts: 1) Rank the importance of each group to your success, using 1-5 (1 being critically important, 5 being of low importance); 2) rank them in order of importance from 1-7 (1 being most important, 7 being least); and finally 3) grade yourself from 1-5 (1 being extremely strong, 5 extremely weak) on how well you intentionally build strong relationships with each of those groups.

This exercise typically helps people realize how reliant each of us is on the other groups, and it applies not only to customer relationships but also to a wide range of internal and external relationships, many of which we might underestimate or take for granted. This exercise also helps us evaluate how well we are working at relating to each of these groups; and, finally and most importantly, it forces us to create a plan to build and measure our key relationships.

| Critical Success Relationships | Importance to My Success | Order of Importance | Strength of Relationship |
|---|---|---|---|
| Customer | | | |
| Suppliers/ vendors | | | |
| Manager | | | |
| Coworker | | | |
| Employees | | | |
| Other departments | | | |
| Outside advisor/ consultant | | | |
| Network/friends | | | |
| | **1-5**<br>1 = Critically Important<br>5 = Low Imortance | **1-7**<br>1 = Most<br>7 = Least | **1-5**<br>1 = Extremely Strong<br>5 = Extremely Weak |

*Your Relationship Report Card helps people realize how reliant each of us is on the other groups, and it applies not only to customer relationships but also to a wide range of internal and external relationships*

## The ABCs of Business—Always Be Connecting

As noted in chapter 1, a study by the Relational Capital Group found that 89 percent of executives believe that relationships are the most important factor in their success year over year. Yet only 24 percent of those leaders actually do anything intentionally to promote relationship building. Finally, less than 5 percent of organizations actually have any specific strategies for helping their professionals develop and strengthen the relationships required to achieve their goals.[1]

As discussed in chapter 5, FORD systems are used by many TDG clients to develop relationships. Collecting and retrieving FORD (family, occupation, recreation, and dreams) is a first easy step; it's low-hanging fruit. Creating FORD systems should not add cost or complexity to your organization's customer experience. All FORD systems should meet the following criteria:

1. Low or no cost: A FORD system needn't cost anything but coaching your employees to pay attention.

2. Simple to execute consistently: Everyone's job is hard enough; we don't want to complicate or add complexity to a person's workload.

3. Has zero impact on productivity: Collecting FORD should not add any time to a phone call, appointment, or checkout transaction.

4. Creates an immediate WOW for the customer: It should be a pleasant surprise to the customer and one that they won't get anywhere else.

Let's examine some of the ways companies have instituted systems for building relationships with their customers.

## Tracking FORD

You can look at anyone's schedule for the day, week, or month and see the customers they interacted with, either over the phone or face-to-face. We launched "February FORD" month at John Robert's Spa to remind everyone of the importance and benefits of focusing and tracking our customers' FORD. At the end of each day, management would check for additions and updates to the FORD notes in the profile of each customer seen that day. Every week we posted results for everyone to see at each location and on our internal Facebook page. The person with the highest FORD percentage (number of customers seen who had FORD information recorded divided by number of total customers seen) received a $100 bonus. In the end we had to pay out several bonuses, because numerous people got 100 percent, meaning they posted FORD notes on every single customer they came in contact with for the entire month of February.

The benefits of tracking FORD were many:

- For the vast majority of our customer-facing employees it became a habit that has continued.

- Employees built better and more rewarding relationships by focusing on what was happening in the customers' lives.

- Our new customer retention rates for the month of February broke all-time records.

## Obsessing Over the Customer

The Select Group (TSG) is one of the leading IT recruiting and staffing companies in the country. Founded in 1999 and based in Raleigh, North Carolina, with 13 locations across the United States and Canada, TSG has more than 200 corporate employees and more than 1,700 consultants serving their customers. As a client of The DiJulius Group, TSG focuses on making the customer experience its number one competitive advantage to avoid having to compete in price wars. Founder and CEO Sheldon Wolitski is the driving force responsible for helping TSG go from zero in sales to over $150 million.

Asked what's behind TSG's success, Wolitski says, "It's obsessing over our customers. We've got two customers. We've got the customers (clients hiring TSG's consultants), and we also have our consultants. We've got over 1,000 consultants that are actually onsite with our customers. I went out and hired a CXO (Chief eXperience Officer), and his whole role is to make sure that customers are having an amazing experience. It's been an absolute game changer. We are just obsessed over this, and it's interesting. It's actually given all of our employees a little bit more of a purpose in life as well, and a purpose in their job. Before, we were focused on revenue and placing people, but now we are focusing on impacting lives, and that's really what we've done. It's really kind of the 'why' behind why we do what we do, so it's been a huge transformation."[2]

> I went out and hired a CXO (Chief eXperience Officer), and his whole role is to make sure that customers are having an amazing experience. It's been an absolute game changer. We are just obsessed over this, and it's interesting. It's actually given all of our employees a little bit more of a purpose in life as well, and a purpose in their job.

The Select Group has implemented FORD both internally and externally. While their new hires are in training, they go over FORD and how they can use it with their clients. However at the same time, TSG is collecting FORD information on the new hires themselves. They then send this information out to branch leadership so they can utilize FORD when their new hires start working in the branches.

For clients, TSG collects FORD information through a template in their tracking system so anyone looking at the record can see the FORD information. "We changed 'family' to be 'favorites' so as not to ask any sensitive demographic info," says Jeff Zirker, TSG's CXO and a graduate of the 2016 class of our Customer eXperience Executive Academy.

## Using Technology to Build Customer Rapport

We've all had the experience of pulling up to a clunky speaker at a fast-food restaurant, shouting out an order, and struggling to understand the voice on the other end. It often gives you the feeling that the drive-thru employees are not very engaged or friendly. However, many quick-service restaurants (QSRs) have found a way to get rid of the annoyance of ordering at the drive-thru with a face-to-face interaction in the form of a video screen. It allows the customer and the employee to chat in full view of each other while placing an order. You don't have to wonder if the server is smiling; you can see her smile. It's all about that customer-employee connection.

Other companies have used a video signature in email—a quick video of 30–60 seconds embedded in an email signature that serves as a more personal introduction. In short, it puts "a face to the name." It also allows a customer to learn about your FORD, which tells them you are a real person with a family and hobbies. It's a great differentiator when you consider how much of your client interaction probably occurs only via email.

## Virtual Engagement

Virtual calls are another big trend. They help build stronger relationships among those who use conference calls—customer service reps, call centers, consultants, and other professionals. Imagine your customers having the ability to click a button on your website to have a virtual call with your customer service rep. It might be that only the customer can see the employee, or they might be able to see each other.

At The DiJulius Group it is standard practice to make all conference calls as video calls. Seeing someone face-to-face forces employees to stay engaged; they can collect client intelligence by seeing what's in a person's office—for example, pictures on their walls. It also ensures my employees (and I) will not be distracted or multitasking while on the call and increases the amount of smiling, friendliness, and attention.

> Seeing someone face-to-face forces employees to stay engaged; they can collect client intelligence by seeing what's in a person's office—for example, pictures on their walls. It also ensures my employees (and I) will not be distracted or multitasking while on the call and increases the amount of smiling, friendliness, and attention.

## Tell Me Something Good

Most people typically start conversations by asking, "How are you?" That can be a dangerous question, however. Certain people will use the question as an opening to vent, telling you everything that is wrong in their world, from "I have been sick for the last three weeks," to "We had to put our dog of 16 years down yesterday." These kinds of responses move your conversation to an unpleasant place and make it hard to recover.

Author and sales coach Steve Nudelberg has a great way to avoid getting into these situations. He encourages people to start every conversation with "Tell me something good." This forces the conversation to start on a positive note. When I have used this as an opening, it not only always gets an upbeat response, but it also delivers great FORD in the answers. For example, I might hear, "My son Jason just graduated from American University."

> This forces the conversation to start on a positive note. When I have used this as an opening, it not only always gets a positive response, but it also delivers great FORD in the answers.

Shirley Crossan, director of guest relations at Supercuts and a 2016 graduate of our Customer eXperience Executive Academy, has shared how her company implemented FORD and helped build positive relationships with customers right from the start. Crossan came up with a list of open-ended questions. Some examples are:

1. What kind of FUN things do you have planned?

2. Tell me the BEST thing(s) that took place since you were here last.

3. Give me some AWESOME news.

4. Where's the most INTERESTING place you've been recently?

5. What's the BEST thing that happened to you before you got in my chair?

6. What's been your FAVORITE part of today so far?

7. Tell me all the GOOD news you've had since your last visit.

8. What EXCITING things are happening in your life?

Crossan boasts about the benefits she has found by gathering and utilizing FORD. "Happier guests return more often," she says, "recommend us to others, post favorable online reviews, and spend more in the salon. Relationships that last are meaningful for all. The salon environment is more fun. Engaged staff that are happier make more money. And finally we reduced staff and guest turnover!"

> Happier guests return more often, recommend us to others, post favorable online reviews, and spend more in the salon. Relationships that last are meaningful for all. The salon environment is more fun. Engaged staff that are happier make more money. And finally we reduced staff and guest turnover!

## Scaling Your Network

Verne Harnish, guru to the fastest-growing companies in the world and author of *Scaling Up: How a Few Companies Make It . . . and Why the Rest Don't,* says what helped accelerate his career when he first started out was the advice he got from Regis McKenna. "It was McKenna, author of the classic *Relationship Marketing,* who taught Steve Jobs, Andy Grove, and most of the Silicon Valley tech stars how to market in the 80s," Harnish says.[3]

McKenna's advice was to make a list of the top 25 (or 250

depending on the size of your business) influencers you need to help scale your business. Influencers are anyone who is instrumental to growing your business. They can include key relationships, customers, potential customers, investors, key employees, well-connected executives, entrepreneurs, mentors, referral sources, and professional experts. Once you have your list, now you need to spend time each week figuring out how to network your way to these people and create a plan to convince these influencers to help you.

> Once you have your list, now you need to spend time each week figuring out how to network your way to these people and create a plan to convince these influencers to help you.

What did this advice do for Harnish? "Being young and dumb and a recent grad of Wichita State University, the top people on my list were President Ronald Reagan, Steve Jobs, Michael Dell, and the owners of *Venture* and *Inc.* magazines," says Harnish. "What's crazy, in just 36 months of working the list, one hour per week, my company at the time, the Association of Collegiate Entrepreneurs (ACE) became a global 'overnight' success, hosting a major event in Los Angeles for over 1,100 entrepreneurs that included none other than Steve Jobs and Michael Dell in attendance. What also helped was the full-page ads we were able to run for the organization, donated by *Venture* and *Inc.* magazines, and a congratulatory telegram from President Reagan."[4]

## ImageFIRST = CustomerFIRST

ImageFIRST is the largest and fastest-growing provider of healthcare laundry services to medical practices throughout the United States.

What accounts for its success? It's the fanatical approach the firm takes in its customers' experience. To start with, the drivers who deliver their products to the customers (that is, hospitals) are called "customer advocates" instead of delivery drivers.

It's not an empty title. ImageFIRST trains its customer advocates to build real relationships with each of its customers by electronically embedding FORD into all prospect- and customer-contact systems. For example, when a sales person is connecting with a potential customer, they can easily gather information and add it to their contact database, which can be seen by any employee who works with that customer. The customer advocate can add information as they service the client, and anyone working at ImageFIRST has access to this information on his or her clients.

"We also developed something called 'FORD Acts,'" says Jay Juffre, executive vice president at ImageFIRST and a graduate of the 2016 class of our Customer eXperience Executive Academy, "where we encourage and recognize our team members who act on the information they have gathered. We built our training at all levels to teach the team how to stealthily gather the information. We can also run reports to see how much FORD information we have on every one of our key contacts."

## The Humanity Factor

Cedar Brook Group, a wealth-management firm headquartered in Cleveland, Ohio, promulgates a philosophy called The Humanity Factor that honors the individual client and emphasizes that he or she is the central figure in the financial-planning process.

Here is how the Cedar Brook Group describes The Humanity

Factor: "Anyone can chase return or market financial products. In contrast, The Humanity Factor is about learning who you are as an individual, husband, wife, or parent; as a leader, mentor, or philanthropist. It's about your relationships, your life's work, your passions, and your contributions. It's about the families, the advisors and the firm working together toward a common purpose: to honor you as the central figure of your own planning. Only when we know who you are, can we prudently and wisely advise you on where to go."[5]

This philosophy seems to be working well for Cedar Brook Group, as they have become one of the largest independent wealth-management firms in northeast Ohio, recognized as one of the "50 Best Places to Work for Financial Advisors" across the nation.

## Be That Memorable Moment

ATI Physical Therapy, headquartered in Chicago, has more than 800 therapy clinics nationwide and is a consulting client of The DiJulius Group. ATI is not your typical physical therapy clinic; its CEO, Dylan Bates, is obsessed with his company's patient experience, and he has a bold vision for transforming his team members. "We want to be disruptive in the physical therapy industry," Bates says. "We want to be a world-class hospitality company that provides great physical therapy by being the highlight of their day." Granted, that sounds more like a day spa than a physical therapy clinic. But that doesn't stop Bates and ATI from being committed to changing the way their patients look at physical therapy. I would say it is having a pretty good impact, as ATI is one of the fastest-growing physical therapy chains in the United States.

Their service vision statement is "Be That Memorable Moment" in a patient's day. And one of the key ways they do this is through a principle that team members live by, called "We Emotionally Invest" (in our patients). They have taken that literally by adding a section with that heading in their patient database. It's a space for clinicians and front-office personnel to enter patients' personal information. Jane Cobler, director of transformation at ATI and the leader for the patient experience project, notes, "Our clinical staff has access to the database daily. Here they can document FORD, and the information carries over visit to visit. It is tied to the patient's master ID, so if the patient returns in the future for a new care episode, the information will continue to carry over into the new chart. This information is also available to our Patient Intake Team, so the front office staff can provide the same type of patient experience, be it over the phone or in person."[6]

## A World-Class Speaker Experience

Every fall, for the past 10 years, The DiJulius Group has produced the Customer Service Revolution, a two-day conference focused on teaching more than 700 executives from around the world how to build a world-class customer service organization. You would assume that the attendees are our primary customers. However, the top customers that we need to make happy are actually the speakers. Every year, we offer a new lineup of more than 15 sought-after speakers.

We know that if we have amazing presenters, we will have no problem filling the room with executives who are eager to learn how to become the brand customers cannot live without. Fortunately, we have a two-year waiting list of speakers who want to present at the Customer Service Revolution.

Why? Because we work hard at providing such an incredible "speaker experience" that past speakers are happy to refer us to great colleagues. Nicole DiGiulio is one of The DiJulius Group employees committed to the speaker experience. Her job, which she does spectacularly, is to blow the minds of the speakers before, during, and after the Customer Service Revolution conference. Nicole is adept at sending brilliantly personalized gifts to speakers ahead of time. Here are some examples:

- Sally Hogshead, author of *Fascinate: How to Make Your Brand Impossible to Resist,* received a necklace with the word "fascinate" in her favorite colors.

- Tim Gard, a hilarious motivational entertainer, uses a rubber chicken as one of his key props in his presentations. He received rubber chicken cufflinks.

- Daniel Pink, bestselling business author and a huge Washington Nationals fan, received Nationals cufflinks and a bag of his favorite candy, Swedish Fish.

- Arnie Malham loves cigars, so we got him a custom humidor with his book logo and name etched on it.

- David Avrin received a NAU (Northern Arizona University) dad's shirt, because his daughter goes to school there.

- Harley rider Neen James received Harley-Davidson champagne flutes.

## The FORD Monthly Allowance

Benson Kearley IFG (BKIFG), headquartered in Toronto, Canada, is not your typical insurance agency, because Stephen Kearley is not your typical company president. BKIFG is obsessed with providing a world-class experience to both customers and employees, and it is paying huge dividends with exponential growth. BKIFG created an amazing incentive to help its team focus on collecting customers' FORD. This program provides every account executive a $25 allowance that they *must* spend every month on their customers. The program reminds employees to listen and recognize customers' FORD and follow up with delightful surprises. For example, an existing customer might call to ask a question about a policy and in the process mention that it's their wedding anniversary this weekend. The comment might trigger the BKIFG employee to send flowers or a gift card.

> This program provides every account executive a $25 allowance that they *must* spend every month on their customers.

BKIFG also came up with a campaign targeted at increasing the amount of customer intelligence they collect on their clients. Back when one of the new *Star Wars* movies was being launched, their slogan was: "May the FORDS be with you!" They even created *Star Wars* advent calendars for each office location. Every day they drew names of associates to open the doors on the calendar. They also had an R2-D2 trophy that was awarded to the top FORD producer.

## We Perform at Our Best When We Make a Personal Connection

Author Daniel Pink has written a great blog about the power of making things personal. Pink cites a study of radiologists in Israel whose job was to read scans on computers. The radiologists were divided into two groups. The first group read scans as usual. The second group also read scans as usual, but they were given a photo of the patient for each scan. The latter group wrote longer, more meticulous reports. "That was interesting," says Pink, "but further into the study, it got *really* interesting. After a period of time, the researchers went back to the group who had been given the pictures of the patients and, without them being aware, had them read the same scans as before but without the pictures. The stunning finding was that about 80 percent of the previous findings were not reported!"[7]

> After a period of time, the researchers went back to the group who had been given the pictures of the patients and, without them being aware, had them read the same scans as before but without the pictures. The stunning finding was that about 80 percent of the previous findings were not reported!

Think about that. Most people believe the customer is the one who benefits when the employee makes a personal connection. But this example clearly shows that when the employees—in this case, the radiologists—have a personal relationship with the customer, they do a better, more thorough job.

## The Five Es

It's not enough to tell your employees to be present or to provide genuine hospitality. You have to tell them how. Make it black and white, and make it measurable. One of my favorite hospitality systems for making a customer connection face-to-face is to fulfill the "five Es." They take less than five seconds to execute, and the first three can even be done simultaneously in just one second. They are:

1. Eye contact

2. Ear-to-ear smile

3. Enthusiastic greeting

4. Engage

5. Educate

## EYE CONTACT

This eliminates the head-down, uncaring, robotic greeting of a front-line employee who just says, "Next." A great training method to teach eye contact is to audit the employees by periodically asking them, "What was the color of the customer's eyes?"

## EAR-TO-EAR SMILE

A smile is part of the uniform, and a real smile shows teeth. Demonstrate a positive attitude and let the customers know that you are happy to serve them.

## ENTHUSIASTIC GREETING

Your greeting must exude genuine warmth. It should demonstrate enthusiasm in the voice, coupled with a smile and eye contact. We need to offer genuine hospitality as if the customer was an old friend visiting our home.

## ENGAGE

Many companies provide little direction to employees on how to engage a customer. This doesn't mean having a 10-minute conversation. Every single customer can be engaged within the time it typically takes to serve them, whether that's 90 seconds in the fast-food environment, 2 minutes on a phone call, or 45 minutes in a meeting. Engagement shows customers that they are individuals. It eliminates being too task-focused on a transaction and replaces that approach with real interaction. Start by using your name and the customer's name. Utilize any customer intelligence you have: information from a database, a name badge, a picture of their twins on the desk, a hat, college shirt, tie, or glasses. Do anything else that helps you connect with the customer.

## EDUCATE

Every single time a customer comes in contact with you, they must leave with the feeling, "No one knows more about what they do than that person."

The five Es are simple to accomplish. They can be executed with the majority of customers, they demonstrate genuine hospitality, and finally, practically no one else is doing them even 25 percent of the time. The five Es also apply to professional service providers or internal customer service, support, or call-center environments.

## Educating Versus Selling

The best brands teach their employees to educate customers rather than sell to them, and I can vouch for how well this works. As I've said, I love technology. The moment some new device is released I have to have it, though I know that is the worst thing a consumer can do. When Apple released a new iPad, I ran into the Apple Store to upgrade mine. I told the employee I currently had an iPad but wanted the iPad 2. He could not have had an easier sale. However, he asked me what I used my iPad for. I said, "For email, surfing the internet, social media, and to read articles and books on it." Then he asked, "Do you play games or watch movies?" "No, never," I replied. Surprisingly he said, "Don't get it. It won't be worth it. The big difference between the iPad and iPad 2 is the resolution and graphics that you would only appreciate if you played games or watched movies."

> He wasn't about making a sale, he was about educating me and making sure I got the right product for my needs.

I couldn't believe he was talking me out of spending $600. I was actually bummed! I said, "Well, maybe I will start playing games." No, seriously, I would have bought anything in the store from this employee after that. He wasn't about making a sale, he was about educating me and making sure I got the right product for my needs.

## Make Your Interview Process Ungameable

The biggest problem with the typical interview process is that most intelligent candidates can game it. Everyone knows they are going to get asked, "Tell me two negatives about yourself." A well-prepared candidate will respond, "I am a perfectionist and workaholic." The companies that hire the best have the best screening processes that are "ungameable."

The following are three best practices for the interview/screening process.

## PUT THEM IN DISTRESS

A great way to test someone's character is to observe how they react when things don't go according to plan. Walt Bettinger, CEO of Charles Schwab, takes every candidate out for a breakfast interview. What the potential employee is not aware of is Bettinger has asked the restaurant to purposefully mess up the candidate's order. As Bettinger sees it, character is everything, and the "wrong order" test is meant to gauge how a potential hire deals with adversity. "It's just another way to look inside their heart rather than their head," says Bettinger.[8]

## THE ENGAGEMENT INDICATOR

If you are looking for people who have the potential to be customer-centric service providers, evaluating their five Es might be your most powerful tool. Many of our consulting clients have incorporated the five Es into their interview process, literally counting the times a candidate demonstrates each one.

For example, they might record the number of times during the interview that:

Eye contact was made                     _____

Ear-to-ear smiles took place             _____

Enthusiasm was displayed                 _____

Engagement with the interviewer occurred naturally    _____

Educated answers were given to interview questions    _____

While I believe most employee candidates have the potential to provide excellent customer service, not all do. The five Es can help you identify candidates who are able to achieve a high service aptitude with rigorous training.

During the interview process, if candidates are not smiling, making eye contact, and showing enthusiasm, then pass. No amount of customer service training will change them. As for the engagement indicator, the key to that is having an interviewer who constantly displays all five Es.

## GROUP INTERVIEWS

In our own businesses, John Robert's Spa and The DiJulius Group, we have found group interviews are extremely productive and telling. The first round of interviews are always with a group of candidates. This reduces the time from six hours with each candidate to one hour. This initial interview starts with what the company is about, what the position is about, and what it takes to be successful at both. We then ask the candidates questions that each have to take turns answering. The potential hire thinks what they are being judged on is who has the best answer, but what we are really observing is what the other candidates are doing when it is not their turn to answer. Are they disengaged or fidgety? Or are they listening, nodding, and smiling while the other person is answering the question. That is the one we want.

## 3-2-1

Once you have established great relationships with your customers, you need to maintain them. An excellent technique for reconnecting with existing and past clients is having your account executives do the following on a weekly basis:

- Send out 3 emails to clients.
- Send out 2 cards to clients.
- Call 1 client on the phone.

The 3-2-1 system is best used for simply connecting with—not selling to—existing or past customers. It is an out-of-the-blue act without any solicitation of product or services, just a random communication ideally using past FORD. For example, you might write, "Hey, Jason, I saw that your Chicago Cubs are in first place and having a terrific season so far. That is great. I hope you and your family are enjoying the summer. Clients like you are one of the reasons why I love what I do." The key is to schedule 3-2-1 on the same day, same time every week. It takes less than 10 minutes.

> The 3-2-1 system is best used for simply connecting with—not selling to—existing or past customers.

## Relationship Killers

We have spent a lot of time on how to build client relationships. The following is a list of actions to avoid that can slowly erode those relationships.

## NEVER USE THE WORD "NO." ALWAYS FOCUS ON WHAT YOU CAN DO

Eliminate the word "no" from your company's vocabulary; no one should ever be allowed to use that word. You may not always be able to say yes, but you can offer alternatives and options. You will be amazed at how creative your team will get at satisfying customers.

> You may not always be able to say yes, but you can offer alternatives and options. You will be amazed at how creative your team will get at satisfying customers.

When someone asks if you can sell them something you don't stock, you can answer with, "While we do not carry product X, what we do carry is product Z, and the reason we carry product Z is because it is proven to be the best, longest-lasting, healthiest whatever . . . " By the time you are done explaining the benefits of product Z, that customer should never want product X. If for some reason they persist, then explain how and where they can get product X.

The book *The Effortless Experience* explains, "'No' is a trigger that sets in motion an entire chain of negative emotions. It's not about explaining why the customer can't have what they want (which is a recipe for increased escalations and sometimes four-letter words from customers), but rather focusing exclusively on what solutions are possible."[9]

> "No" is a trigger that sets in motion an entire chain of negative emotions. It's not about explaining why the customer can't have what they want but rather focusing exclusively on what solutions are possible.

The authors recommend creating an "Experience Blueprint," which is "designed to explore and uncover a customer's primary motivation for their request—to learn what's really going on in their mind—and then suggest available alternatives that are likely to be just as satisfactory as the initial request. So while alternative positioning is not a silver bullet, it is effective in taking much of the negativity and pain out of calls, not just because it allows more customers to have a lower-effort resolution experience, but because it also mitigates at least some of the worst, most emotionally draining calls frontline reps have to deal with every day."

## NO NEED TO OVER-SHARE. JUST OWN IT

Employees sometime over-share. Why? Because they want to make sure the customer knows whatever happened wasn't their fault. How often have you heard: "I didn't know you were here. The receptionist never informed me. If I had known, I would have been out sooner." Or "Shipping didn't next-day-air the package . . . I put it on the order . . . They do this type of stuff all the time." Does the customer really need to know who screwed up and why? All they need to know is how sorry we are about what happened and what we are going to do to make it right. If we need to address something internally, that's our business. Our customers do not need to know about our dirty laundry. It doesn't matter whose mistake it was. We just handle it and make it right.

> Does the customer really need to know who screwed up and why? All they need to know is how sorry we are about what happened and what we are going to do to make it right.

## NEVER RUSH THE CUSTOMER. ASK IF THERE IS ANYTHING ELSE YOU CAN DO

I love this line, which can be used in every single customer interaction in every business—on the phone, face-to-face, checking someone out, or via e-mail: "Is there anything else I can do for you today?" While an employee may have three other customers waiting for help or 40 emails in their inbox, just saying, "Is there anything else I can do for you?" makes that customer feel as if they are your only concern.[10] We encourage all the contact centers we work with to incorporate this question in the close of their conversations.

## The Self-Absorbed Barometer

When having a business conversation with a customer or potential customer, I try to keep the focus of the conversation entirely on them, using the FORD technique. The more I can keep asking them questions, the more I learn about them, the happier they are, and the more they end up liking me. When a customer asks me a personal question, I will answer; however, I try to be brief and eventually steer the conversation back to them.

Using the FORD technique on a personal level is different. It lets me know if I want to invest time in the future with the other person. I can't tell you how many times I meet someone for the first time socially and FORD them for a while. The person always seems to enjoy answering my questions. However, after we are done talking, they probably couldn't tell you one detail about me. They never ask me one question. They don't know what I do for a living, if I have kids, zero. When this is the case, I know this is probably not someone I want to spend more time with in the future.

One time my significant other, Claudia, and I had dinner plans with one of her friends and the friend's husband, Arthur, whom I had never met before. So I did what I always do and I used the FORD technique and found out that Arthur loves to fly-fish. Now fly-fishing is not something I have ever been interested in. Still, for 90 minutes, Arthur told me everything I didn't want to know about fly-fishing. Three positive things came out of that conversation:

> I can't tell you how many times I meet someone for the first time socially and FORD them for a while. The person always seems to enjoy answering my questions. However, after we are done talking, they probably couldn't tell you one detail about me.

1. Arthur had a great time at dinner, which made his wife happy and earned me points with Claudia.

2. I actually didn't hate learning about fly-fishing as much as I thought I would, mostly because of how much passion Arthur had for it.

3. Around three to four months later, I was meeting with a CEO who was considering hiring The DiJulius Group. On the wall in his office was a picture of him fly-fishing. Based on what I had learned from Arthur, I was able to speak to him with some knowledge about his hobby. It helped me make a stronger connection with that CEO, and he eventually became a client of ours.

## What about People Who Don't Want to Be FORDed?

Not every customer you deal with wants to build a relationship or is willing to allow you to make a connection. It is important to read the person. Some take longer; you'll need more interactions before they feel comfortable enough to let their guard down. Others may simply want a transaction, chop-chop. That is perfectly okay. If someone appears to prefer minimal interaction, we can do that; but I find they're only a small percentage of customers. Typically people who prefer a transaction are only looking for the "best deal" they can find and end up being short-term customers at best.

Companies that flourish in the Relationship Economy attract a higher percentage of clients who value doing business with a brand that demonstrates not only expertise but also genuine caring. They are looking for companies that they can trust, who will always do what is in the best interest of their customers.

## Accumulate Relationships

Keith Ferrazzi, in his book *Never Eat Alone*, says it best, "Wherever you are in life right now, and whatever you know, is a result of the ideas, experiences, and people you have interacted with in your life, whether in person, through books, music, email, or culture. There is no score to keep when abundance leads to even more abundance. So make a decision that from this day forward you

> Wherever you are in life right now, and whatever you know, is a result of the ideas, experiences, and people you have interacted with in your life . . . So make a decision that from this day forward you will start making the contacts and accumulating the knowledge, experiences, and people to help you achieve your goals.

will start making the contacts and accumulating the knowledge, experiences, and people to help you achieve your goals."[11]

> *"Life is relationships; the rest is just details."*
> —GARY SMALLEY

## CHAPTER 6 TAKEAWAYS

- How do companies and their leaders know where they stand on their most important business relationships? By making reliable, effective systems that enable employees to consistently work at the development of their relationships and assess their progress.

- Your Relationship Report Card helps people realize how reliant each of us is on the other groups, and it applies not only to customer relationships but also to a wide range of internal and external relationships.

- Seeing someone face-to-face (virtually) forces employees to stay engaged; they can collect client intelligence by seeing what is in a person's office. It also ensures you and your employees will not be distracted or multitasking while on the call and increases the amount of smiling, friendliness, and attention.

- Make a list of the top 25 influencers you need to help scale your business. An influencer is anyone who is instrumental to growing your business. Once you have your list, you need to spend time each week figuring out how to network your way to these people and create a plan to convince these influencers to help you.

- Implement the FORD Monthly Allowance, which provides

every account executive a dollar amount that they must spend every month on their customers.

- Train your employees to execute the Five Es when having face-to-face customer connections—eye contact, ear-to-ear smile, enthusiastic greeting, engage, and educate.

- Educating versus selling—it is not about making a sale, but rather educating the customer and making sure they buy what is right for their needs.

- The 3-2-1 system is best used for simply connecting with—not selling to—existing or past customers.

- Using the word "No" is a trigger that sets in motion an entire chain of negative emotions. It's not about explaining why the customer can't have what they want, but rather focusing exclusively on what solutions are possible.

# BE THE BRAND CUSTOMERS
# CANNOT LIVE WITHOUT

> *"You do not merely want to be considered just the best*
> *of the best. You want to be considered the only one who*
> *does what you do."*
>
> —UNKNOWN

We all have a company or two that we can't live without. Which company would you hate to hear this about: "You can never do business with them again"? When I ask my audiences this question, the same brands typically are mentioned: Apple, Starbucks, Nordstrom, American Express, and Amazon. The more important part of the question, though, is: Why? All these companies have competitors that offer identical products and services for less. What have those brands done to make customers feel they can't live the rest of their life without them? That is brand loyalty. That is

> The more people feel like they cannot live without your brand, the closer you are to making price irrelevant.

power. The more people feel like they cannot live without your brand, the closer you are to making price irrelevant.

## Are You an Expendable Line Item on a P&L?

If you are a business that serves other businesses (B2B), someone's vendor, for example, then you are always in danger of being replaced. As you know, every company, including yours, constantly examines its budget and reviews expenses for the year. CEOs are always demanding that their leaders find ways to trim their costs and improve their bottom line. Therefore, you and your company are either: 1) a line item on the P&L that can be outsourced to the lowest bidder, or 2) a non-negotiable partner, about whom a key decision maker will say, "I don't care what we have spent with them; it doesn't come close to the value we get in return. We are not switching."

There's a business metaphor about a CEO under attack. The CEO has a foxhole to retreat to, but he can only bring three vendors into it with him. He has to choose the three he couldn't afford to lose if he had to start all over tomorrow. He doesn't care about the rest. He knows he can replace those easily, probably more cheaply. When it comes to your clients, you need to ask yourself, would you be in the CEO's foxhole?

How do you become a non-negotiable partner? I don't care what you sell; there are dozens of companies that sell the same thing. The way to stand out is to know your clients' business and industry better than they do. You need to understand what is keeping them up at night. You need to provide so much value that anytime they need to make an important decision, they think of you, even if what they are looking for is outside your area of expertise. They have to have the confidence that you will know someone who will know the answer. You need to be their most trusted advisor.

## How to Be the Trusted Advisor Your Clients Can't Live Without

Charles Penzone is a longtime friend and owner of one the most successful salon operations in the United States. I will never forget something shocking he once said to me: "I hope I die before my banker does." He went on to say, "It isn't just his advice and expertise. I never make a decision without consulting with him first. If I were thinking about painting the walls of my office a different color, he'd be the first person I would ask. I am pretty sure he doesn't know a thing about paint, but I know he will find out who does. When he found out I was looking for a new accountant, he introduced me to the three best in the city. I hired an excellent receptionist he recommended. I cannot fathom life without him." The way Chuck talked about his banker means that banker is definitely in Chuck's foxhole, and it made me want to find some key professionals in my stable of vendors that I could feel similarly about.

Trusted advisors or consultants are resource brokers. They understand the power of relationship building and making the right connections and introductions. They know how to uncover what their client needs even when their client doesn't know them yet.

Being a trusted advisor means demonstrating that no one cares about your

> Being a trusted advisor means demonstrating that no one cares about your customer's business like you do. You earn business by being generous with your knowledge and resources without asking for anything in return.

customer's business like you do. You earn business by being generous with your knowledge and resources without asking for anything in return. Your clients will never share their problems with you until they trust you. As billionaire Mark Cuban says, "The best salesperson is the one the customer trusts and never has to question."[1]

> "My goal is to make my client look like a hero to his organization and customers."

Here are a few specific guidelines for becoming a customer's most trusted advisor:

1. Love what you do. People can't fake passion. Passionate professionals are magnets, and customers love to buy from people who have an incredible amount of positive energy for what they do and whom they do it for.

2. Get to know your customer not only professionally but also personally. Know their FORD by making an emotional connection with them that eventually builds into an unbreakable relationship.

3. Be more committed to the success of your customer than they are. That may mean you refer them to someone else and lose the sale.

4. Don't share how you can help them until you have completely understood what their goals and problems are. In any conversation the client should talk at least 80 percent of the time.

5.  Make sure your clients never meet anyone smarter than you at what you do. Read every book and relevant article on your subject. Your learning never stops.

6.  Be honest and transparent. You are the expert, and it is your responsibility to advise your client to do what is in their best interest, even when that may go against what they think they want.

7.  Go ugly early—share bad news as soon as you can.

8.  Be a resource broker. Make the right connections and introductions.

## Show Me You Care More about Helping My Business Than Getting My Business

Larry Gould is a life insurance advisor. I met him back in 1998, after the first business I started, John Robert's Spa, was featured on the front page of the business section of our daily newspaper because of our rapid growth.

Larry walked into our corporate offices a few days later. Nobody had ever seen him before. He said he saw the article in the paper, and as a congratulations gift, he presented us with the story on a beautiful metal plaque. Immediately suspicious, I asked, "What's your pitch?" He said, "Nothing, I just want to congratulate you. I love to see young people succeed."

After that Larry started coming in once a month for a haircut. It was always a pleasure to see him; Larry knows a lot about many things—business, family, and people—and he brought a great deal of positive energy with him every time he visited. One time he asked me, "John, would you mind if I purchased $50 spa gift cards for some of my top clients?" I said, "Do I mind? Of course not."

I was embarrassed I didn't even know what Larry did for a living. I asked him, and he said, "I help people save money and take care of their family through some vehicles I provide, such as life insurance, estate planning, and numerous other ways." I had already heard that same line from dozens of insurance salesmen but never from someone who had given me so much first.

Larry knows the secret of making people want to do business with him. He talks about what interests them and about how to help them get what they want. His interests or desires never enter the conversation. He also doesn't ask for your business. He gets the other person to ask what he does. Eventually I bought a small term-life policy because I needed it and because I wanted to give Larry the business. He had more than earned it.

Over the course of two decades, Larry has taken my entire family and me to dinner several times. He has attended my son's wrestling tournaments, has never missed attending my annual Customer Service Revolution conference, and for nearly 20 years, he has dropped off pastry every Friday at each of our salon locations and corporate office. Most importantly, Larry is a personal friend who is always full of great advice and encouragement.

As a result of Larry's way of doing business, I have to admit I am probably the most over-insured human being. His approach has me constantly thinking, "How can I give him more of my business?" It makes me wonder how many of my clients think, "How can I give John more business?" And how many of your clients think that way about your company?

When I met Larry back in 1998, he was 72 years old. At the time of writing this book, he is 93 and still working, active, and sharp. What's the secret of his success? He says, "If you have a client who needs a job, then help him with a resume and introduce him to your contacts. If you know someone who is looking for funds, then introduce him to potential investors. If you know someone who is looking for an employee, then help him find a key person. If you know someone who is looking for a loan, then fix him up with a banker. Be a resource for people. Learn to help people first, long before you ever ask for the sale."[2]

> If you have a client who needs a job, then help him with a resume and introduce him to your contacts. If you know someone who is looking for funds, then introduce him to potential investors. If you know someone who is looking for an employee, then help him find a key person. If you know someone who is looking for a loan, then fix him up with a banker. Be a resource for people. Learn to help people first, long before you ever ask for the sale.

> *"Trust is about relationships. I will trust you if I believe that you're in this for the long haul, that you're not just trying to maximize your own short-term benefits."*
> —DAVID MAISTER[3]

## Relationship Building, Not Networking

The trusted connections one has built up over time are known as "social capital." It acts as a human library of resources we can access anytime to gain or share information, knowledge, advice, and introductions. Social capital is a result of long-term, continuous relationship-building and one of the most powerful resources a person can have. You build social capital by always putting the other person's goals first and foremost in every business relationship.

Lewis Howes, author of *The School of Greatness*, refuses to network. "I just connect and add value," he says. "Networking is more transactional. It's more focused on getting a result for yourself as opposed to thinking of how can you be of service to the other person in front of you that you meet and genuinely have interest in their needs as opposed to your needs." [4]

> Social capital is a result of long-term, continuous relationship-building and one of the most powerful resources a person can have. You build social capital by always putting the other person's goals first and foremost in every business relationship.

Connecting is about finding out what the other person needs and how you can help. According to Keith Ferrazzi, "The words networking and networker can suggest a self-serving purpose: that you're in it to see what you can get out of others. A connector is reaching out to form an alliance with the other person, offering to be of service first and foremost. Networkers like to work the room and collect cards, but those cards don't really mean much if the other person isn't willing to take your calls because all you did was schmooze and move on." [5]

"Connector" is exactly how I would describe Sheldon Harris, Partner at CEO Coaching International, a leading coaching firm for growth-focused CEOs and entrepreneurs, and a former president/CEO of many successful companies. Sheldon and The DiJulius Group share many of the same clients. One of the most impressive testimonials I repeatedly hear from CEOs who work with him is, "He is the best hour of my week." What a way to be thought of!

Everything I have described about being a trusted advisor and connector applies to Sheldon Harris. It seems like a week doesn't go by where I don't receive an email from him introducing me to one of his clients for one reason or another. Often he will say his client's business is growing really fast and needs help with customer experience. Or he might just make an introduction and say, "I am not sure why, but I think the two of you need to meet." I trust Sheldon and find every one of his introductions to be beneficial. Sometimes they lead to new business for The DiJulius Group; sometimes the other party and I realize that we can help each other. What impresses me the most is how Sheldon is always thinking of ways he can add value to his clients. In every business relationship his focus is on the other person's goals first and foremost.

## It Is Better to Be Their Favorite Than the Best

Think about the companies you frequent the most. They may be your favorite local restaurant, cafe, hair salon, or dry cleaner. Even if some of them screwed up, you would immediately forgive them because of the emotional equity they have built up with you. Now consider why you are so loyal. In most cases it is because they have gotten to know you well. All the employees and the other regular customers know you. And you know the employees by name. You are part of a community.

If I had to choose, I would rather be my client's favorite than be known as the best. Why? Being the best is subjective; however, being someone's favorite is not—it is a fact, their fact. How does a company become a favorite? They get to know their customers. The best companies do it by design, not by chance, not out of eventual familiarity. They train their employees to develop relationships by making emotional connections, even with new customers, on every interaction.

## Making Price Irrelevant

When you say you want to make price irrelevant, it sparks conversation and debate. Is it possible to actually do that? Absolutely! But that does NOT mean that you can double your prices or raise them 20 percent tomorrow and not lose a customer. What it does mean, though, is that based on the experience your business consistently provides to your customers, they have no idea what your competition charges.

Typically, for the majority of companies we do business with, we know how much they charge and whether we can get the same thing from somewhere else for the same cost or less. However, we all have a few businesses we are loyal to because of something that they repeatedly do for us or because of how they make us feel. In those cases, we have no idea what their competitors charge, nor do we care.

> Making price irrelevant means that based on the experience your business consistently provides to your customers, they have no idea what your competition charges.

Every business has to decide where they want to compete—in the price wars or the experience wars. I prefer to compete on the basis of customer experience. There's a lot less competition. Many times when a customer complains about the price, it isn't because they were not willing to pay for something; it is because the experience didn't warrant it. Price is something you offer when you have nothing else.

However, I do believe in price guarantees. How can that be? Am

I a hypocrite? Not at all. A blog post written by Jeff Shore, titled "Don't Wage a Price War," inspired me.[6] A paradigm shift is needed from selling a commodity someone can get anywhere to an experience customers can only enjoy with your company. Everyone in your organization needs to have this mentality: "We are the premium experts and ultimate experience provider. We will not be oversold. In fact if you can find it more expensive somewhere else, we will raise our prices and match it."

> Everyone in your organization needs to have this mentality: "We are the premium experts and ultimate experience provider. We will not be oversold. In fact, if you can find it more expensive somewhere else, we will raise our prices and match it."

Sound crazy? Well, if that truly was the mind-set of everyone in your company, it would change your approach to the experience you provide. It would force us to deliver the ultimate experience. Personally, I would get upset if I found out that someone was charging more for something my business sells. That doesn't mean I would just raise our prices. First we would have to figure out what they are providing that we aren't. Is it quality, consistency, or an experience? Then we would need to improve our game—make it better than anyone else's. Once we did that, we would be able to charge the most and be proud of what we charged relative to the total experience we delivered.

## What Value Do Your Employees Place on Your Services?

Ask your employees this question: If your customers told you that they could get what you sell from someplace else for significantly less, what would you do to keep them? You will probably be disappointed at your employees' answers. Too often when faced with that scenario, employees act apologetic and start offering the customer more. Or even worse, they discount to justify the price gap. The problem is, your customer-facing employees may not understand the true value of the services and products they are selling to the customer.

> Too often when faced with that scenario, employees act apologetic and start offering the customer more. Or even worse, they discount to justify the price gap. The problem is, your customer-facing employees may not understand the true value of the services and products they are selling to the customer.

How good a job are you doing at creating the perception of value for the expertise and experience of your services? How well is this value articulated to your employees? Remember that the value your employees perceive is going to be projected to your customers. Do you sell a commodity similar to your competitor, or are you the premium expert and experience provider? Doing business with your company should mean the customer has peace of mind about the expertise and quality you provide.

## Discounting Is the Tax You Pay for Being Average

Are your customers an incentive away from going elsewhere? If they are, you have nothing. You have no customer equity. There is always someone who can make something a little crappier and sell it a little cheaper. That's why it is a mistake to act as if cheap imitators are your competition and to play into their hands by reducing your prices. You are only giving them credibility and removing

> There is always someone who can make something a little crappier and sell it a little cheaper. . . . If you feel your products and services are superior, then your prices should reflect that.

yourself as the leader of your industry. If you feel your products and services are superior, then your prices should reflect that. Everyone expects to pay more when they are dealing with the best. But when the best is similar in price to the rest of the pack, customers get suspicious, the perception of excellence disappears, and you are left with merely a commodity.

One of the best benefits of building strong relationships with customers comes when you inevitably screw up. Customers are so much more forgiving and understanding of mistakes if you have built a relationship. When something doesn't go right, you have a golden opportunity to demonstrate to your customers that you pose zero risk to them. What does zero risk look like? As a customer, it means you are sure that when you deal with a company and something goes wrong, they will make it right.

> **What does zero risk look like? As a customer, it means you are sure that when you deal with a company and something goes wrong, they will make it right.**

## An Opportunity to Be a Hero

When a problem arises with a customer, it gives us the opportunity to own that customer for life. I have always had a saying in my businesses, "If it gets to me, it is free." This was meant to make sure all my employees, including those on the front line, take care of anything that arises. No one wants to contact the GM or call the owner. If they do, clearly the situation has gotten out of hand. I also have a saying: "You will never get in trouble for something you do, only for something you don't do." Meaning: Just take care of the customer. Be naive instead of paranoid. Trust the customer.

> *"Don't punish 98 percent of your customers for what you are afraid 2 percent might try to do."*

One of my favorite all-time customer service recovery stories happened several years ago when I was involved day-to-day in my first business, John Robert's Spa. A client called me to tell me one of my hairdressers had gotten hair color on her blazer. I apologized and offered to pay to get her blazer cleaned. The client said it could not be cleaned; the stain was permanent. I again apologized and offered to replace the blazer, but she said it was part of an outfit no longer available, and the outfit was worthless now that the blazer was ruined. I told her I would put a check in the mail for the cost of the outfit. She was stunned and told me it cost $250 and asked if I wanted to see the blazer or receipt. I told her neither was necessary and she seemed extremely happy. After we hung up, I looked up her history in our computer system and found that she had been coming to our salon about seven times a year for the last several years. I also noticed she had never referred anyone. So I sent her the check and included a John Robert's gift certificate for the trouble and inconvenience that we had caused.

About a year later, I was curious if we had retained her. When I looked her back up, I saw that she was still coming regularly. However, I was shocked to see she had also referred 18 new customers that year. What kind of advertising could I buy for $250 that would

> I was shocked to see she had also referred 18 new customers that year. What kind of advertising could I buy for $250 that would get me 18 new customers? I told all my stylists to start spilling color on everyone's clothes!

get me 18 new customers? I told all my stylists to start spilling color on everyone's clothes!

## While It Is Not Your Fault, It Is Your Problem

I took my son Johnni to Disney World when he was six years old. We both stood in line for the Twilight Zone, one of the Disney-MGM Studios rides, for more than 50 minutes. When we finally got to the front of the line, the staff member stopped us because Johnni was too small for the ride. He showed me the measuring stick, and we saw he was right. For my son's safety, he had to be at least 40 inches high. My son was almost 2 inches too short. The staff member apologized and said we must have missed the signs along the line. We really couldn't argue, but after waiting in line for almost an hour for a ride he really wanted to go on, Johnni was about to cry.

The Disney employee bent down to my teary-eyed son, asked his name, and said, "I am going to give you a certificate with your name on it. This certificate says the next time you come to Disney, you will probably be tall enough to get on Twilight Zone and you won't have to wait in line. All you have to do is walk right up to the front of the line, show this certificate, and you'll go on the ride without waiting."

> **What Disney gets that most companies don't is while it isn't their fault, it *is* their problem.**

My son's expression turned into a smile. He felt like a Disney VIP. The staffer seemed to be about 20 years old, which amazed me. With the service aptitude I had at 20, I would most likely have said, "Dad, get your whiny kid out of my face. It isn't my fault he isn't tall enough. It isn't my fault you somehow missed the five signs saying how tall he needs to be. This happens to me several times an hour, and I'm sick of it. Why do I need to fix this?" However, what Disney gets that most companies don't is while it isn't their fault, it *is* their problem. Instead of going home and remembering the long lines, how hot it was, how much money we spent, and how we couldn't get on one of the rides, we had this certificate hanging on our refrigerator door for the next two years. Every day Johnni would say, "Can we go back to Disney today?" I would measure him and say, "Not yet."

> *"While they may complain about the service defect, they will rave at how well we handled it."*

## It Is Rational for Customers to Be Irrational

When emotions are involved, logic disappears. Emotions pour out, manipulate our reasoning, and lead to action. It's no accident that customer experience can trigger a wide array of emotions that can have a great influence on repeat business. Sometimes we don't know why we like going to a certain place, yet nevertheless something drives us to stop there. We may try to find a logical excuse, perhaps pointing to convenience or some other factor. But the truth is, the business delivered a unique experience that leaves a subconscious impression. On the other hand, negative thoughts about a brand are often caused by a poor experience that left a permanent blot in our memory.

It can be confusing and frustrating for employees when customers react unreasonably to something that seems minor. However, when a customer has expectations—not unrealistic expectations, but simple ones about what it will be like to do business with you—and the business fails to deliver, the customer can get emotional. Even though it may have been the first time the company messed up, the customer may still react irrationally.

Daniel Kahneman, a psychology professor at Princeton, is a Nobel Prize winner for his research proving we behave emotionally first, rationally second. As human beings, our emotions are the most powerful factor in how we respond and interact with others.[7] For that reason, it is critical that dealing with customer emotions—especially for dissatisfied customers—becomes part of employee service-recovery training. Once employees understand there is a good probability of a customer reacting emotionally instead of rationally, they won't take it personally and will be better able to make a brilliant comeback. The watchword for employees should be QTIP—Quit Taking It Personally.[8]

> Once employees understand there is a good probability of a customer reacting emotionally instead of rationally, they won't take it personally and will be better able to make a brilliant comeback.

> *"When dealing with people, remember you are not dealing with creatures of logic, but creatures of emotion."*
> —DALE CARNEGIE

## Relationships Left to Chance Will Always Be Vulnerable

One of my favorite books is *The Compound Effect* by Darren Hardy, which is based on the premise that decisions shape your destiny. One story Hardy shares is a real eye-opener, and it applies to relationships, both personal and professional. Hardy relates how, when he was 18, a seminar about personal accountability in relationships transformed his life. The speaker had asked the audience, "What percentage of shared responsibility do you have in making a relationship work?" Hardy was confident he knew the answer. He shouted, "Fifty/ fifty!"

"It was so obvious; both people must be willing to share the responsibility evenly or someone's getting ripped off," Hardy explains in his book. "'Fifty-one/forty-nine,' yelled someone else, arguing that you'd have to be willing to do more than the other person. Aren't relationships built on self-sacrifice and generosity? 'Eighty/twenty,' yelled another."[9]

"The instructor turned to the easel and wrote 100/0 on the paper in big black letters. 'You have to be willing to give 100 percent with zero expectation of receiving anything in return,' he said. 'Only when you're willing to take 100 percent responsibility for making the relationship work will it work. Otherwise, a relationship left to chance will always be vulnerable to disaster,'" Hardy continues.[10]

> "You have to be willing to give 100 percent with zero expectation of receiving anything in return," he said. "Only when you're willing to take 100 percent responsibility for making the relationship work will it work. Otherwise, a relationship left to chance will always be vulnerable to disaster."

"I quickly understood how this concept could transform every area of my life," writes Hardy. "If I always took 100 percent responsibility for everything I experienced—completely owning all of my choices and all the ways I responded to whatever happened to me—I held the power. Everything was up to me. I was responsible for everything I did, didn't do, or how I responded to what was done to me. You alone are responsible for what you do, don't do, or how you respond to what's done to you."[11]

Hardy's conclusion still resonates: "This empowering mindset revolutionized my life. Luck, circumstances, or the right situation wasn't what mattered. If it was to be, it was up to me. I was free to fly. No matter who was elected president, how badly the economy tanked, or what anybody said, did, or didn't do, I was still 100 percent in control of me. Through choosing to be officially liberated from past, present, and future victimhood, I'd hit the jackpot. I had the unlimited power to control my destiny."[12]

One of my favorite philosophies is "everything is our problem." Regardless of whose fault it is (the customer's or ours), when something goes wrong, it is our problem. We have to own it; we have to figure out how to build such an incredible intuitive experience that eliminates the majority of potential issues or addresses them immediately, regardless of whose fault it may be.

## Love in the Business World

Let's talk about a word that is not used regularly, or comfortably, in the corporate world. That word is "love." The word may be unspoken, but in the end all executives want people to *love* their brand. They want their employees to *love* working for them. We want our customers to *love* us.

Think about the top brands in the world. People don't buy from Starbucks, they *love* Starbucks. People *love* Apple, Zappos, Lululemon, and Amazon. You may *love* your hairdresser, your account executive, your manufacturer, or distributor. But why? What did they do to make you *love* them?

All relationships begin with a connection. It may be a momentary interaction prompted by the first three of the five Es (eye contact, enthusiastic greeting, and ear-to-ear smile). It might grow through engagement and education. Soon your customer will come to realize the connection is not about the sale; rather you are truly interested in what's best for them.

Falling in love with your brand is not possible until the customer feels that they are the most important person in the relationship, and that it is all about them. As we've discussed, you need to take the time to acquire customer intelligence and learn about their FORD. When you've built a strong relationship, the customer will not be able to imagine a world without your business. You now have a brand evangelist, a customer who loves your brand and tells everyone they know how amazing you are. That is better than any marketing you could ever pay for.

> Soon your customer will come to realize the connection is not about the sale; rather you are truly interested in what's best for them.

I love the phrase that Seth Godin coined, "Out-LOVE your competition." That is the most distinct competitive advantage a company can have. Think about it. Nearly everything can be copied: the products or services that you sell, your décor, website functionality, menu, and prices. Can you really out-work your competition? Can you out-think them? The one area you can get a distinct competitive advantage is by out-loving the businesses you compete against. The only way to do that is stop the typical complaining that goes on about how difficult customers can be and just start appreciating them.[13]

## Start Having Customer Appreciation Meetings

I am not talking about having a customer appreciation event or week, or starting a VIP loyalty program. These are all good practices to implement, but what I am talking about is having internal customer appreciation awareness campaigns. This will dramatically change the mind-set of your employees. Far too many employees discuss how difficult their customers can be, how demanding they are, and how they have unrealistic expectations.

Do you want your employees to be more grateful for the customers they serve? Emphasize the positive. Companies need to create several outlets where employees can hear all the positive stories about their good customers. This will change the tone from *us versus them* to genuine caring about your customers, and make everyone on your team grateful for the customers they have. When enough customers *love* your business, you have just made price irrelevant and have become the brand they cannot live without.

> Companies need to create several outlets where employees can hear all the positive stories about their good customers. This will change the tone from *us versus them* to genuine caring about your customers, and make everyone on your team grateful for the customers they have.

Finally, love has to start at home. In business terms, that means also treating your employees with world-class service. Creating team members who can't live without your brand will create customers who feel the same way. That is the subject of the next chapter.

> *"Love is the most powerful drug. Some people call it passion, purpose, or a calling. However, there is only one common denominator that changes a person to the point where she can't wait for the sun to rise, jumping out of bed in the morning, excited about the day. That emotion is 'love,' whether it's romance, your children, hobby, a cause, product, your customer, or career."*

## CHAPTER 7 TAKEAWAYS

- The more customers feel like they cannot live without your brand, the closer you are to making price irrelevant.

- You and your company are either: a line item on the P&L that can be outsourced to the lowest bidder, or a non-negotiable part of your customer's life.

- Being a trusted advisor means demonstrating that no one cares about your customer's business like you do. You earn business by being generous with your knowledge and resources without asking for anything in return.

- Focus on building relationships versus networking.

- Social capital is a result of long-term, continuous relationship-building and one of the most powerful resources a person can have. You build social capital by always putting the other person's goals first and foremost in every business relationship.

- Making price irrelevant means that based on the experience your business consistently provides to your customers, they have no idea what your competition charges.

- Every business has to decide where they want to compete—in the price wars or the experience wars.

- Your customer-facing employees may not understand the true value of the services and products they are selling to the customer. What they perceive is going to be projected to your customers.

- What does zero risk look like? As a customer, it means you are sure that when you deal with a company and something goes wrong, they will make it right.

- Don't punish 98 percent of your customers for what you are afraid 2 percent might try to do.

- While it isn't their fault, it is their problem.

- It is rational for customers to be irrational. Once employees understand there is a good probability of a customer reacting emotionally instead of rationally, they won't take it personally and will be better able to make a brilliant comeback.

- Companies need to create several outlets where employees can hear all the positive stories about their good customers. This will change the tone from *us versus them* to genuine caring about your customers, and make everyone on your team grateful for the customers they have.

# BE THE BRAND EMPLOYEES CANNOT LIVE WITHOUT

> *"When I hire someone, it is at that time*
> *I go to work for them."*

I have had the good fortune to work with many great leaders of successful companies. One of the best of them is Admiral Thomas Lynch, who served in the US Navy for 31 years. He was also the captain of the Naval Academy's football team and the center for Heisman Trophy award winner Roger Staubach. Admiral Lynch serves as the executive chairman of NewDay USA, a mortgage company for active service members, veterans, and their families. NewDay is one of our longtime consulting clients, allowing me the opportunity to see his leadership firsthand. The mantra he has lived by since his early days in the navy is "Ship, Shipmate, Self."

A sign at the Naval Academy reading *Non Sibi Sed Patriae* originally inspired Lynch. Translated from Latin, it means: "Not for self but for country." "I first walked through those doors in the summer of 1960 as a freshman (plebe) at the Academy," Lynch says.

"Those words above the door had a lasting effect upon me. It calls for one to subordinate their own interest in a selfless pursuit of serving others. It's only through such a commitment of self-sacrifice that one can realize fulfillment as a boss, officer, parent, or leader. From the moment I accepted my Naval Academy appointment, I hoped to serve others—to serve the country."[1]

"Throughout my life, I would use this fundamental message to both motivate and measure myself," Lynch explains. "This concept was built on the premise that no thought, deed, or action would be taken without first thinking: 'How does this impact our ship, then my shipmates and then self?' Both individual and global success could be realized through a collective pledge of selfless sacrifice. This system of leadership would draw upon the natural impulse of people to want to be part of something greater than one's self—to find gratification by contributing to a cause that serves others."

> This concept was built on the premise that no thought, deed, or action would be taken without first thinking: "How does this impact our ship, then my shipmates and then self?" . . . This system of leadership would draw upon the natural impulse of people to want to be part of something greater than one's self—to find gratification by contributing to a cause that serves others.

Lynch's leadership style can and should be applied across all companies. It speaks to the need that all of us have to feel we work for more than a paycheck, more than ourselves, but for some greater organization. Author Robin Sharma puts it this way, "Leadership is about relationship. The best leaders build strong social networks and rich communities of teammates, suppliers, and customers that will help them get to where they're going (while they, in turn, reciprocate).

And world-class leaders know how to connect. Find ways to connect: With the people you work with. With the loved ones you live with. And with the strangers you share this journey called life with. You'll not only attract more professional success. You'll feel more personally significant."[2]

## Employees Do Not Quit Companies, They Quit Managers

Studies have shown that the reasons people leave their jobs are directly related to how connected they feel at work. The Family and Work Institute has found that compensation and benefits have only a 2 percent impact on job satisfaction, while quality and workplace support have a combined 70 percent impact.[3] Retaining employees is not a function of the human resources department. Employees are most engaged when they feel as though their work is important, they are appreciated, they learn and grow, and they feel a part of a great team.

> The single most important determinant of an individual's performance and commitment to stay with an organization is the relationship that individual has with his or her immediate manager.

In fact, the single most important determinant of an individual's performance and commitment to stay with an organization is the relationship that individual has with his or her immediate manager. People leave their manager far more often than they leave the organization.[4]

The cost of replacing an employee is somewhere between 1.75 to 2.5 times his or her annual salary. Moreover, high turnover can cause remaining employees to question their own loyalty.

Author Rob Markey wrote astutely about "The Four Secrets to

Employee Engagement" for the *Harvard Business Review* and shared some startling data from a Bain and Company study that surveyed 200,000 employees:

- Engagement scores decline with employee tenure, meaning that employees with the deepest knowledge of the company typically are the least engaged.

- Engagement scores decline as you go down the organization chart, so highly engaged senior executives are likely to underestimate the discontent on the front lines.

- Engagement levels are lowest among sales and service employees, who have the most interactions with customers.[5]

All three findings are cause for concern; however, the most serious conclusion is the last one—that the people who deal with your customers the most have poor or no engagement.[6]

> All three findings are cause for concern; however, the most serious conclusion is the last one—that the people who deal with your customers the most have poor or no engagement.

## The Currency for Millennials Is Purpose

It's true millennials pose unique challenges for businesses: first, how to lead them as employees, and second, how to attract them as customers (which we will address in chapter 9). In both cases, companies need to understand what motivates millennials. Managers love to complain about how difficult it is to employ this generation, blaming them for poor customer service. My experience as an employer has been the opposite. I have found in The DiJulius Group and John Robert's Spa, where we have a large percentage of customer-facing millennial-generation employees, that this group delivers outstanding customer service consistently! In many cases, the younger generation is better at delivering genuine hospitality than older generations who grew up with less technology and therefore had more face-to-face human interactions.

Why do some companies have a large, unmotivated, and apathetic workforce, while other excellent companies boast a workforce willing to make ridiculous sacrifices to achieve customer satisfaction? One answer may be that they select better candidates. However, I truly believe only a small fraction of people are born with the "service DNA." Great companies with great leaders and a strong, uncompromising culture are responsible for creating a totally engaged workforce.

> When it comes to the millennial generation, it's important to know they're not interested in trading hours for dollars. They want to be part of something big, part of a purpose.

When it comes to the millennial generation, it's important to know they're not interested in trading hours for dollars. They want to be part of something big, part of a purpose. Think of companies like Zappos, Chick-fil-A, Nordstrom, The Ritz-Carlton, and Disney. All of these companies employ millennials who are fully engaged in their work. The businesses that tie job responsibilities to an overall purpose and bigger picture get incredible results from millennials—and also from the rest of their employees.

## Employees Would Rather Be Criticized Than Ignored

According to a Gallup poll on the "State of the American Workplace," when bosses completely ignore employees, 40 percent of staffers actively disengage from their work. When the boss criticizes on a regular basis, 22 percent of employees actively disengage. So even if employees are being criticized, they are actually more engaged; they feel that at least someone is acknowledging that they exist! And if bosses recognize just a single strength and reward employees for doing what they're good at, only 1 percent actively disengage from the work they are expected to do. Added to those statistics is the fact that people who go to work unhappy actually do things, actively or passively, to make those around them unhappy, too.[7]

> People who go to work unhappy actually do things, actively or passively, to make those around them unhappy, too.

Again, leaders who have a relationship with their employees will find that their staff is more effective. So when we help companies work on creating a world-class internal culture and better leadership skills, we always do an internal FORD (family, occupation, recreation, and dreams) exercise with the leadership team. We give them a list of the employees who report directly to them and see how much FORD they know. For example, do they remember the spouse's name, spouse's occupation, and names and ages of kids? Sadly the majority of leaders struggle with this. Yet as leaders, one of our primary responsibilities is to actively build strong rapport with our employees.

Even what appears to be a little thing to us may be huge to younger team members—their first car, for example. Do you remember your first car? Mine was a total beater that shouldn't have been allowed on the road; however, it was all mine. Getting that car was more special to me than driving a fancier car off the showroom floor years later.

## Leadership Means Connecting with Colleagues and Customers

On January 3, 2019, beloved Southwest Airlines co-founder, rebel, and innovator Herb Kelleher died. *Forbes* magazine said, "Kelleher was perhaps the best CEO in America." Southwest has had 46 years of consecutive profitability in an industry where horrible customer service is the norm, an industry with deplorable employee morale and where turning a profit is next to impossible. Southwest has thousands of employee evangelists rarely seen anywhere else and is one of the most-referenced and iconic customer service brands.

"Herb created a culture that inspires passionate people to come to work fully awake, fully engaged, firing on all cylinders because they know they are doing epic work," write Kevin and Jackie Freiberg in the *Forbes* story. "The reason the people of Southwest Airlines have such a strong affection for Herb Kelleher is pretty simple. First, he was an incredible listener. When you were with Herb, he was 100% all there—totally engaged. He made you feel like you were the most important person in the world at that moment, and to him you were."[8]

> When you were with Herb, he was 100% all there—totally engaged. He made you feel like you were the most important person in the world at that moment, and to him you were.

Want to know how well a leader is creating high employee morale? Ask employees to rank their direct leader on the following three questions on a scale of 1-5 (5 being the highest):

1.  Does this leader care about the company?

2.  Does this leader care about my success?

3.  Does this leader care about me as a person?

Perception is reality. If the average score from your employees is less than a 4.5 for any of those three questions, you have work to do—and it is clear in which area.

## Email Eliminates Brainstorming

People working in the same offices, literally three cubes apart, email or message each other. All this is much more productive but eliminates any possibility of having a conversation that can lead to unpredictable paths and creative collaboration, not to mention opporutunities for employee engagement and leader's recognition of doing their job well.

## World at Your Service

Celebrity Cruises' service vision statement is the "World At Your Service." Given that philosophy, it is no surprise that they have been selected as "Best Premium Cruise Line." Celebrity understands that service must be experienced on the inside—by the employees—long before it can ever be experienced on the outside. Jonathan Meyer, manager of customer experience, explained Celebrity's commitment this way: "During a Celebrity internal culture workshop our leadership team was asked point blank: 'How well do you really know your team?' The overwhelming answer was 'Very well, we've worked together for years. We have a great relationship.' Then they were asked to write down all the FORD information they knew about their direct reports. The first three points of FORD are very straightforward, however not one leader could fill in the dreams and future aspirations of their direct reports."[9]

> To really get to know a person on a deeper level by learning their hopes, dreams, and aspirations—this elevated level of trust is what we are all aiming for. When trust within our team reaches this point, that's really when the magic happens.

Meyer adds, "To really get to know a person on a deeper level by learning their hopes, dreams, and aspirations—this elevated level of trust is what we are all aiming for. When trust within our team reaches this point, that's really when the magic happens. High trust is at the core culture of all successful companies, and low trust comes at a really high price. The FORD method was introduced as a tool to elevate relationships and build trust within our teams, applicable to everyone from the VPs in the head office all the way to our Celebrity Cleaners onboard all of the ships. No matter the title or position, we really felt like the FORD method should be utilized and promoted with every single one of our team members."

Celebrity included FORD in the computer-based training program they use to certify each Celebrity employee on the company's service philosophy. They also included the FORD method as an integral part of their leadership team's one-on-one's, employee check-in, and quarterly review sessions. Meyer concludes, "We are confident that by focusing on our internal culture, elevating the trust within our teams and making a true commitment to service excellence we will continue yielding positive results in guest ratings, revenue, and employee satisfaction."

## No One Rises to Low Expectations

I was a horrible student when I was growing up. I was diagnosed with Attention Deficit Disorder and it was recommended that I repeat every grade in elementary school. For whatever reason, my mother wouldn't allow it. Still, I was a handful for my teachers to deal with.

When I was in fourth grade, my mother attended a parent-teacher conference and when she came home, she lectured me about what my teachers had said. When she was finally done listing everything the teachers complained about, I asked, "Did they say anything nice about me?" My mother paused and said, "They said you always look nice." Looking back now, I know that wasn't true. I was a sloppy kid. I had long messy hair, my clothes were ragtag hand-me-downs, and I am pretty sure I only showered once a week.

I am positive my mother made up the compliment, but it had a tremendous impact on me. The next morning getting ready for school, I took longer getting dressed and doing my hair because I felt I had a reputation for "looking nice" that I had to live up to. I can't imagine what might have happened if I'd been told, "John shows amazing potential in math."

> "As leaders we are in the human development business."

## Energy Givers vs. Energy Suckers

Science has proven that energy is exchanged between people every time we come into contact with each other. We literally give and receive energy. But that can happen in two ways. You can be an

"Energy Giver," bringing positivity and leaving people feeling better for having interacted with you, or your negativity drains them, and you are known as an "Energy Vampire," also called energy suckers.

I love what Mark Moses, founding partner of CEO Coaching International, says: "The CEO is the Chief Energizing Officer." In fact, the greatest leaders are the best energy givers all of the time. Their presence can change a room. After conversations with these types of leaders, employees get excited about themselves and the critical part they play in the company's success. Leaders with energy make those around them better.

> Science has proven that energy is exchanged between people every time we come in contact with each other. We literally give and receive energy. But that can happen in two ways. You can be an "Energy Giver," bringing positivity and leaving people feeling better for having interacted with you, or your negativity drains them, and you are known as an "Energy Vampire."

Ask yourself if you are an energy giver or an energy sucker. Just because you high-fived someone this week doesn't make you a full-time energy giver. You have to do it consistently. It has to be a conscious decision, an intentional choice.

Energy Givers:

- raise the confidence of everyone they come in contact with
- improve morale, chemistry, and performance
- constantly show gratitude and thanks
- give everyone else the credit
- believe in others
- are there for others when they struggle, fail, or are going through hard times

- are their employees' biggest cheerleaders
- constantly find out what their employees' goals are and help them achieve those goals
- are great listeners
- always build strong relationships and build emotional capital with those around them
- will walk through fire for those on their team
- give more

It is just as important to reflect on the type of people around you. Are you surrounding yourself with energy givers or energy vampires? How do they compare to the list above? Are you hiring and promoting energy givers?

> *"The moment you became a leader you lost the right to make excuses. The moment you became a leader, it stopped being about you."*

## Nothing Ruins a Company's Customer Experience Faster Than Rapid Growth

Rarely does a company go through rapid growth without having their customer experience suffer significantly. Imagine your company growing, expanding, and needing more employees—a lot more, maybe hundreds more. How picky can you be when you need 400 new employees within the next few months? Locations have to be opened. Demand for your product and services is exploding. The pressure is on to get people hired and trained.

This is where most companies start compromising on whom they hire. Even worse they may start fast-tracking new employees through training. That's a mistake. What has always made you unique are the people you hired, how well they were trained, and the great customer experience your company delivered. If you give in to compromises, you will have high turnover, low morale, and your customer experience will be so inconsistent it will become a liability instead of your strongest competitive advantage.

Growth is great when done right. But don't succumb to the growth trap. You can't compromise your hiring, training, and the customer experience your company delivers.

Getting hired at your company should be extremely hard. It is only fair to your existing employees that you stay extremely selective on whom you let in. People need to earn the right to be a part of your culture and legacy. Your goal should be that every long-term employee considers their decision to join this company as one of the best decisions of their life.

> Getting hired at your company should be extremely hard. It is only fair to your existing employees that you stay extremely selective on whom you let in. People need to earn the right to be a part of your culture and legacy. Your goal should be that every long-term employee considers their decision to join this company as one of the best decisions of their life.

> *"We don't hire people with more winning qualities than anyone else; we just bring out their winning qualities."*

## Hire for Attitude, Not Aptitude

If you want happy employees, hire only happy people. Be picky; hold out for people who ooze service. Negative people are like a virus that spreads quickly. Steve Jobs once said, "It is too easy, as a team grows, to put up with a few 'B' players, and they then attract a few more 'B' players, and soon you will even have some 'C' players. 'A' players like to work only with other 'A' players, which means you can't indulge 'B' players."

Cydney Koukol, chief communication officer of Talent Plus, says something similar, "What happens when you hire amazing people is that they are disappointed when they have to work with mediocre people . . . Every time you select someone, your culture gets better or worse."[10]

> "Most people come to work for a company having had previous work experiences. In many cases, their experience has been bad. As such, they enter with cynicism, and the burden of proof is on leaders to demonstrate that this is a different place."
>
> —HOWARD SCHULTZ

If you waste a lot of time with high-maintenance employees, you end up neglecting the quiet, unsung heroes who deserve your attention.

Hiring new employees should not be your top priority. Instead focus on creating an amazing internal culture with high morale and low turnover. High employee attention will produce high employee retention, which is much easier and less expensive than recruiting new employees. Be careful where you are giving your attention, however. If you waste a lot of time with high-maintenance employees, you end up neglecting the quiet, unsung heroes who deserve your attention.

> *"Days of lighting fires under people are over.*
> *Days of lighting fires inside people are here."*

In his bestselling book *When: The Scientific Secrets of Perfect Timing*, Daniel Pink says, "Once a group is operating in sync, member's jobs aren't done. Group coordination doesn't abide by the set-it-and-forget-it logic of the Crock-Pot. It requires frequent stirring and a watchful eye. That means to maintain a well-timed group you should regularly ask these three questions:

1. Do we have a clear boss—whether a person or some external standard—who engenders respect, whose role is unambiguous, and to whom everyone can direct their initial focus?

2. Are we fostering a sense of belonging that enriches individual identity, deepens affiliation, and allows everyone to synchronize to the tribe?

3. Are we activating the uplift—feeling good and doing good—that is necessary for a group to succeed?"[11]

> *"Human beings rarely go it alone. Much of what we do—at work, at school, and at home—we do in concert with other people."*
>
> —DANIEL PINK

Collaboration is a critical business strategy. The trend of the past decade has been to allow employees to work from home virtually. However, that results in less collaboration. And when collaboration is down, creativity is down, which results in fewer ideas shared, less brainstorming, and less employee buy-in or. new products and services created. Innovation evaporates.

## Great Leaders Are Great Storytellers

As Daniel Pink points out, "One way that groups cohere is through storytelling. But the stories your group tells should not only be tales of triumph. Stories of failure and vulnerability also foster a sense of belongingness."[12]

Nearly every company has rags-to-riches stories about someone who started off in a frontline position and today is in senior management. These stories need to be shared with new employees. Most new employees are overwhelmed with the information overload and the insecurities of being a novice; they cannot fathom being a rock star someday. Hearing about someone who struggled early on and went on to great success can be really inspiring to a new employee early in his or her career.

"Among all the attributes of the greatest leaders of our time, one stands above the rest," says David Horsager, author of *The Trust*

*Edge: How Top Leaders Gain Faster Results, Deeper Relationships, and a Stronger Bottom Line.* "They are all highly trusted. You can have a compelling vision, rock-solid strategy, excellent communication skills, innovative insight, and a skilled team, but if people don't trust you, you will never get the results you want."[13]

Horsager teaches leaders how to build and maintain trust through developing the following strengths:[14]

> Most new employees are overwhelmed in their early days with the information overload and the insecurities of being a novice; they cannot fathom being a rock star someday. Hearing about someone who struggled early on and went on to great success can be really inspiring to a new employee early in his or her career.

- Clarity: People trust the clear and distrust the ambiguous. When leaders are clear about expectations, they will likely get what they want.

- Compassion: People put faith in those who care beyond themselves. Think beyond yourself and never underestimate the power of sincerely caring about another person.

- Character: People notice those who do what is right ahead of what is easy.

- Contribution: Few things build trust quicker than actual results. Be a contributor who delivers real results.

- Competency: People have confidence in those who stay fresh, relevant, and capable. The humble and teachable person keeps learning new ways of doing things and stays current on ideas and trends.

- Connection: People want to follow, buy from, and be around friends—and having friends is all about building connections. Trust is all about relationships, and relationships are best built by establishing genuine connection. Show gratitude—it's the primary trait of truly talented connectors. Develop the trait of gratitude, and you will be a magnet.

- Commitment: People believe in those who stand through adversity.

- Consistency: In every area of life, it's the little things—done consistently—that make the big difference. The great leaders consistently do the small but most important things first.[15]

> *"Great leaders want to make the world a better place, they are willing to do what it takes, make the necessary sacrifices, and rally others to do the same."*

## Be a Dream Maker

One of the privileges we have as leaders is helping others accomplish their dreams. When leaders can help others get what they want—this applies to employees, coworkers, bosses, family, friends, and neighbors—the leaders themselves get what they want sooner and more often. It is so easy to do. Find out what other people around you want and help them get there. Many times it costs nothing. The key is knowing what it is your employees, for example, truly want and connecting them with the right people. Is there any better legacy than helping people accomplish things they never thought possible? The leaders who learn this are always the most successful and fulfilled.

We've incorporated this concept into our businesses. When we hire someone, we have him or her fill out a personnel sheet, which asks things such as favorite flower, restaurant, and "wild ideas" (a kind of bucket list). At managers' meetings, we share this information, so leaders are aware of their team members' personal goals and can take advantage of an opportunity to assist a team member accomplish one of those wild ideas.

> *"The highest honor I receive is the privilege*
> *of helping others achieve their dreams."*

## Engaging the Family of Your Employees

When Dave Timmons was the SVP at Bank of America, he realized the power of family engagement. He says, "I asked one of my team members to head a special two-month-long project. She finished the project under budget, way ahead of schedule, and exceeded my expectations. So I wanted to do something special to thank her."

Dave uses a special form to get to know team members, asking them to share 10 of their favorite things (food, restaurant, shopping center, and so on) or some of their firsts (first car, first concert, and so on). "I knew this team member had a sports team she liked and particular places she liked to shop. However, I wanted to make this recognition extra special because she really deserved it."[16]

Timmons goes on, "About a month after she completed the

project, a letter showed up in this team member's mailbox addressed to her husband, Roger, and their three children, Emily, Shaun and Katrina. It read, 'Dear Roger, Emily, Shaun, and Katrina: I want to tell you how special your wife and mother is. She just finished a project and she is so appreciated at our company that I wanted you to know two things: First, how proud we are of her and how appreciative I am to you for allowing her to take time away from you to work for us. On behalf of our entire team and me, please surprise her with this gift certificate from Ann Taylor Loft, because we know that's where she likes to shop. Sincerely, Dave Timmons, Senior Vice President.'"[17]

Timmons explains, "When you engage the people employees care about, like their family, in their success, you hit a double home run. You can reward them with something—and that's good. But if you want to go for the real wow, try to include their family. It especially gives the kids something nice to remember."[18]

Nothing is more important to anyone than his or her children. Ask your employee how their kids are doing. You can always jog your memory about their names by keeping your employee's FORD updated in your mobile contacts app.

> When you engage the people employees care about, like their family, in their success, you hit a double home run. You can reward them with something—and that's good. But if you want to go for the real wow, try to include their family. It especially gives the kids something nice to remember.

John Ruhlin, in his book *Giftology*, underscores the importance of family by sharing something an early mentor told him: "All of my clients are married and I find that if I take care of the family, everything else seems to take care of itself." Inspired by that, Ruhlin has implemented his own innovations: "Treating our employees well is a top priority, which is why we pay to have their houses cleaned every other week. Happy employees have happy families."[19]

## The Single Best Predictor of Employee Satisfaction

Replying to employees' emails in a timely manner can dramatically increase employee satisfaction, according to Daniel Pink: "When I asked Congressional Chorus artistic director David Simmons what strategies he used to promote belonging, his answer surprised me. 'You reply to their e-mails,' he said. The research backs up Simmons's instincts. E-mail response time is the single best predictor of whether employees are satisfied with their boss, according to research by Duncan Watts, a Columbia University sociologist who is now a principal researcher for Microsoft Research. The longer it takes for a boss to respond to their e-mails, the less satisfied people are with their leader."[20]

It is critical that leaders respond to emails and follow up with employees—just as they would respond to a customer—within 24–48 hours, even if they don't have the answer to the question.

Being a great leader today is tough. You need to be smart, agile, open-minded; the list goes on and on. However, the most critical skill any leader (executive, supervisor, teacher, coach, or parent) needs to master and execute to help others obtain their highest potential is the ability to "Encourage."

## Encourage = In-Courage

The word encourage comes from the old French word *encoragier*, meaning "make strong." Have you ever actually thought about the word "encourage" before? En-Courage = In-Courage. To encourage is to put courage in another person. When you encourage, you are filling another up with courage.

Is your team willing to walk through a fire for you? Have you demonstrated that you would walk through a fire for them? Are you their biggest cheerleader? Are you that person that, when people talk about their success, will talk about the belief you had in them, long before anyone else? Your faith and constant encouragement wouldn't allow them to fail.

## Caught You Doing Something Right

Do you have a system that reminds and inspires you to encourage others on a consistent basis? In my companies, one of the most effective tools in boosting morale is our "Caught You Doing Something Right" card, which acknowledges some specific positive action or behavior a team member has executed. We keep stacks of these cards in the employee break room, call center, and any other room a team member enters. We started using them as a management tool, and now everyone has access to them. An employee may open his drawer and find a "Caught You Doing Something Right" card thanking him for helping someone through a mini-crisis the day before. Most employees collect and save these cards.

Our management team is required to catch people doing something right on a regular basis. This is so embedded in our culture that we now have a spreadsheet with every employee's name down one side and each manager's name across the top. The manager fills in the date he or she last sent that employee a "Caught You Doing Something Right" card. This way we can spot when someone hasn't been recognized in a while and immediately "catch" him or her.

We have even held "Caught You Doing Something Right" contests, and the employee who gives the most cards wins a gift certificate to a nice restaurant. The entire team really gets into it. One shy employee went home one night and wrote out 111 personalized cards to everyone on our staff.

A great lesson I learned from working with The Ritz-Carlton Hotels is how they put all their existing employees through the orientation process again. I immediately brought this idea back to my companies, and we instituted a reorientation for all our existing employees every other year, meaning if you were hired in 2017, you would retake our orientation training in 2019, 2021, and so on. Mixing experienced employees with new hires has had incredible benefits we didn't anticipate. During key points in the orientation, veteran employees shared testimonials, telling stories of what it was like when they joined the company. This immediately created a bond between new and seasoned employees and helped reduce the typical anxiety of being a new employee.

> Mixing experienced employees with new hires has had incredible benefits we didn't anticipate. During key points in the orientation, veteran employees shared testimonials, telling stories of what it was like when they joined the company. This immediately created a bond between new and seasoned employees and helped reduce the typical anxiety of being a new employee.

Most of all, it reinvigorated our seasoned staff. Many experienced employees expressed great surprise at how much the orientation had improved, and they were reinspired by the company's story—where we came from, what it took to get us here, and where we are headed.

## A Crisis Is a Horrible Thing to Waste

Jaime A. Pun, the CEO of Tai Pak's Restaurants, a chain headquartered in Culiacan, Mexico, is a graduate of our 2017 Customer eXperience Executive Academy. In 2012 Tai Pak decided to open four new restaurants, which did not have the success they were hoping for. (Remember, nothing will kill customer experience faster than rapid growth.) The restaurant chain started to struggle financially. Around this time Pun read one of my earlier books, *What's the Secret?: To Providing a World-Class Customer Experience.* "Reading that book was a total game-changer for myself and entire company," Pun says. "Our response to our financial problems was to create a five-year plan based on building a world-class guest and employee experience."

He adds, "We have changed so much of our service DNA as a company, improving our internal culture, improved processes, improved approach on guest experience, that we decided to completely change our brand identity. We launched Tai Pak 2.0, and the main objective was for our guests to rediscover us as a guest-centric company."

## Go, No Go

Tai Pak has integrated FORD into their hiring process. All the information provided during interviews is classified into FORD. "During our World Class Internal Culture workshop we created 'Go' and 'No Go' characteristics of a prospect for each of the FORD components. For instance, a 'Go' for family would be something like the prospect enjoys spending time with his family. A 'No Go' would be the prospect said something negative about his family," explains Pun. "There is a list of five to ten 'Go' and 'No Go' categories for each component of FORD. If a prospect has two or more 'No Go' responses, they are not hired. This has proved to be a very simple yet powerful way of determining if our culture will adopt the prospect easily or not."

One of the main features of Tai Pak's World-Class Leadership training program also has to do with FORD.

> During their monthly one-on-one meetings with their employees, supervisors are encouraged to share their own FORD in order to humanize the relationship and build up trust with one another.

Pun says, "During their monthly one-on-one meetings with their employees, supervisors are encouraged to share their own FORD in order to humanize the relationship and build up trust with one another. They are also required to gather at least one FORD piece each time they meet with a team member. The results are very positive so far. They are building strong relationships."

Is all this stuff worth it? Has it paid off? He says, "We have grown over 60 percent in same-store sales in just a few short years, not to mention the impact it has had on our employee morale and turnover."

## Vulnerability Is a Strong Leadership Trait

In an interview with *The New York Times*, Walt Bettinger, CEO of Charles Schwab, said early on he assumed his employees only cared about themselves and didn't want to hear about him. "But one of the lessons I learned is that, in the transition from management to leadership, I had to open up. I had to be vulnerable. I had to share with people. In fact, it was more important than anything to share with people the great failures in my life as opposed to the successes," said Bettinger.

"Leadership is something completely different. With leadership, you make a decision every day about whether you choose to follow someone. And you make it in your heart, not your head. The ability to inspire followership is so different than management, and it requires transparency, authenticity, vulnerability and all things that are completely unnatural to you when you are trying to build and achieve and accomplish."[21]

## A Culture That Rocks

When it comes to building a world-class internal culture, no one does it better than Arnie Malham, a successful entrepreneur, speaker, and author of a fantastic book called *Worth Doing Wrong: The Quest to Build a Culture That Rocks*. In his book, Malham shares the seven commandments for creating a culture that rocks:

1. Respect your employees.

2. Invest in your employees.

3. Embrace top-down core values.

4. Hire for culture.

5. Generate unavoidable culture. (Go big or go home!)

6. Do it wrong, make it better, get it right.

7. Never give up.

Here are some of the amazing best practices Malham's companies have instituted to create their culture:

- Unrestricted paid time off

- Surprise beer cart (Yes, they hand out beers at work)
- BetterBookClub (paying people to read)
- Free postage for personal mail
- Dream Manager (a program to help employees accomplish their personal dreams)
- Confidential cash advances (no questions asked)

Arnie's sayings are memorable and worth repeating:

- "You don't have a bad culture because you have bad people."
- "If leaders don't do the things they say they're going to do, their company is at a disadvantage."
- "Don't make rules for the masses based on the sins of a few."
- "You don't need everyone to be an A-player in terms of experience; I need A-players in terms of attitude."[22]

## Don't Be a Disney Boss

Maybe you have heard the term "Disney Dad," which refers to a parent who indulges his or her child with gifts and good times but leaves most or all disciplinary responsibilities to the other parent. Too many leaders act in a similar fashion—they're "Disney Bosses."

A Disney Boss is a CEO or president who likes to make an annual big splash, taking the staff to an exclusive resort or giving away hundreds of thousands of dollars and prizes at the company's awards dinner. This definitely gets everyone's attention in the moment. However, for the other 51 weeks of the year, a Disney Boss focuses on what's wrong with his team's performance and barely provides any positive acknowledgment and reinforcement. It's up to the rest of management to do damage control. Ken Blanchard, author of *The One-Minute Manager*, calls this type of leader a "Seagull Manager." He says, "Seagull managers fly in, make a lot of noise, dump on everyone, and then fly out."[23] The vast majority of employees (supported by research studies) will tell you they would prefer more recognition from their leaders. The important thing is the leader's presence, not their presents.

## Invisible Service Providers

A great leader ensures that every single person in the organization realizes how important they are to the company's ability to deliver a superior customer experience. Jeff Toister wrote an interesting blog post titled, "The Outsized Impact of Invisible Service Providers." An invisible service provider is someone at your company who plays an extremely valuable role in your customer experience but rarely if ever actually comes in contact with your customer. They do not get the attention or credit they deserve, and if you ask them to identify their customers, typically they will tell you they don't have any. Nearly every business has invisible service providers—in housekeeping, maintenance, kitchen support, shipping, warehouse, and the home office staff.[24]

> An invisible service provider is someone at your company who plays an extremely valuable role in your customer experience but rarely if ever actually comes in contact with your customer.

It is critical that every business recognize the vital role these invisible service providers play in your customer experience. They can make or break it. And everyone in the company needs to be aware of their significance.

While I was in college, I worked at United Parcel Service as a pre-loader, loading trucks in the middle of the night. I had a customer—the package driver who drove the truck I loaded, the one who had to deliver the packages all day—but no one ever told me that. When I didn't do as good of a job as I could have, the drivers would come in and share their frustration with me, but I just blew them off as jerky coworkers. After graduating from college, I got promoted to UPS driver and finally realized that my success every day was predicated on how well my truck was loaded and organized. Some days it was horrible. I would find packages at 3 p.m. in the back of my truck that should have been delivered at 10 a.m., when I was on the other side of town. Now I had to backtrack, which made me late to the rest of my stops and late getting home. UPS missed a golden opportunity to teach loaders who their real customer was and how we affected their day.

## A World-Class Experience Starts at the Home Office

Most leaders don't do enough to educate their home office team on how they, too, have customers—in operations, in the field, and wherever there are employees who count on them every day to deliver what they need to service their customers. Every employee and department must understand the critical part they play in creating a world-class customer experience. I am not talking about employee engagement or how likely employees are to refer a family or friend. Those are important but have more to do with how good the organization is to work for. I am talking about the experience the home office team delivers to support employees who deal with the invisible service providers in IT, marketing, human resources, accounting, maintenance, and so on.

"Improving the self-esteem of the world" is the purpose statement of Self Esteem Brands (SEB), the parent company of Anytime Fitness, the world's largest and fastest-growing co-ed fitness club chain. Anytime Fitness has been repeatedly named "Best Place to Work," and, indeed, I haven't worked with many companies that can rival the culture created by cofounders Chuck Runyon and Dave Mortensen.

Why? One key reason is they are not solely focused on the member (customer) experience. They are equally obsessed with how their headquarters delivers a similar experience to their franchisees and team members in their 3,800-plus locations. Among other things, Anytime Fitness measures how satisfied their franchisees are with headquarters, just as they do when a member visits one of their clubs. After a franchisee has an interaction with someone at the home office, they may get an email asking them to rate the experience.

This type of accountability is crucial in changing a company's culture and revolutionizing the mind-set of traditional home offices, which too often act like the people from the field or operations are an interruption. "Ongoing stakeholder feedback, consumers, franchisees and employees, is critical for growth and turns shareholders into 'careholders,'" says Runyon.

Whatever the strategies and processes your leadership uses, the goal is the same: to make your company a place employees *love* to work, strengthening your relationship with them, and ultimately ensuring the success of your brand.

> *"Imagine a world where people wake up every day inspired to go to work, feel safe while they are there, and return home at the end of the day feeling fulfilled by the work they do, feeling that they have contributed to something greater than themselves. Fulfillment is not a lottery. It is not a feeling reserved for a lucky few who get to say, 'I love what I do.'"*
>
> —SIMON SINEK[25]

## CHAPTER 8 TAKEAWAYS

- Leadership is about relationship. The best leaders build strong social networks and rich communities of teammates, suppliers, and customers.

- Employees do not quit companies, they quit managers.

- When it comes to the millennial generation, it's important to know they're not interested in trading hours for dollars. They want to be part of something big, part of a purpose.

- Want to know how well a leader is creating high employee morale? Ask the employee to rank their direct leader on the following three questions on a scale of 1-5 (5 being the highest):

1. Does this leader care about the company?

2. Does this leader care about my success?

3. Does this leader care about me as a person?

- The CEO is the Chief Energizing Officer.

- Ask yourself if you are an energy giver or an energy sucker.

- Getting hired at your company should be extremely hard. It is only fair to your existing employees that you stay extremely selective on whom you let in. People need to earn the right to be a part of your culture and legacy. Your goal should be that every long-term employee considers their decision to join your company as one of the best decisions of their life.

- Hire for attitude, not aptitude.

- Every time you select someone, your culture gets better or worse.

- If you waste a lot of time with high-maintenance employees, you end up neglecting the quiet, unsung heroes who deserve your attention.

- When you engage the people employees care about, like their family, in their success, you hit a double home run. You can reward them with something—and that's good. But if you want to go for the real wow, try to include their family. It especially gives the kids something nice to remember.

- Put seasoned employees through new employee orientation again—mixing experienced employees with new hires has had incredible benefits. During key points in the orientation, veteran employees shared testimonials, telling stories of what it was like when they joined the company. This immediately created a bond between new and seasoned employees and helped reduce the typical anxiety of being a new employee.

- An invisible service provider is someone at your company who plays an extremely valuable role in your customer experience but rarely if ever actually comes in contact with your customer.

# ARE YOU BEING DISRUPTED OR
# ARE YOU THE DISRUPTOR?

> *"Be willing to look very differently at your business. Be*
> *willing to look at how to disrupt your business model,*
> *because if you aren't willing to, someone else will."*

Forget about today. Companies that are solely focused on today are in danger of being swept away. To guarantee growth and survival, you better be working on what your customer experience model will look like in the next 5 to 10 years. Why is this important? Because every so often, a product or service comes along that can eliminate other products altogether. Worse yet, there are some examples of a product eliminating multiple industries.

Which of the following products have you owned at one time in your life?

| | | |
|---|---|---|
| Camera | Multiple TV remotes | Wristwatch |
| Wallet | Alarm clock | Board games |
| Flashlight | Calculator | Video games |
| Portable GPS | Calendar/day planner | Kindle/e-reader |
| Garmin for running | Voice recorder | Handheld video recorder |
| DVD player | Seminar workbooks | House phone |
| CD player | Books | Voice mail machine |
| MP3 player | Magazines | White pages |
| Palm pilot | Presentation clicker | Yellow pages |
| Cell phone | Garage door opener | |

I personally have owned every single product on that list. Today, they are all consolidated into one device, my iPhone. I am sure you can think of even more items, devices, and gadgets that have been eliminated by the advent of the smartphone. Originally, Steve Jobs's objective with the first iPhone was to make our lives simpler by combining three major devices—the mobile phone, the palm pilot, and the MP3 (music) player. However, it didn't stop at just those three. Look at the list above and think about how many industries the iPhone has impacted or eliminated. Many of these products, like alarm clocks, flashlights, cameras, and calculators, were necessities that most people don't need anymore.

## Convenience Wins

The iPhone not only did the work of other devices, it did it easily and innovatively. Similarly, making it easy for your customers to do business with you means less hassle, fewer steps, less red tape, fewer explanations, and less redundancy.

How easy and convenient are you to do business with? Your competitor has the same products and services. So all things being equal, how can an organization tip the scale in its favor? Convenience.

Companies like Apple, Amazon, Google, Uber, and Starbucks have shown us how to spoil consumers and have raised the bar for businesses in every industry to follow suit. If you want to win in business, figure out how to be more convenient than your competition by removing traditional bottlenecks that customers are sick of.

> Your competitor has the same products and services. So all things being equal, how can an organization tip the scale in its favor? Convenience. If you want to win in business, figure out how to be more convenient than your competition by removing traditional bottlenecks that customers are sick of.

Hugo Boss has teamed up with Uber to create "Boss On Demand." A car will pick up the client and deliver them to an appointment with a Hugo Boss stylist, allowing them to stay productive, return calls, hammer out emails, and not worry about parking. Hugo Boss will also use Uber for its rush service. Did you spill soup on your shirt at lunch? Hugo Boss can Uber you a new one within an hour. The company also now allows customers to designate a retail outlet to pick up alterations.[1]

## Customer Service Hurts More Than It Helps

A study by the Corporate Executive Board Company found that a company's customer service may do more damage than good if the customer has to put in a great deal of effort during the interaction. Annoying customer service is four times more likely to make customers disloyal instead of loyal.[2] The Customer Effort Score (CES) is a way to measure your customer service by asking a customer how difficult it was to place an order, get an issue resolved, get a question answered, or a problem fixed.

The authors of *The Effortless Experience* argue, "The key to mitigating disloyalty is reducing customer effort. Companies should focus on making service easier, not more delightful, by reducing the amount of work required of customers to get their issues resolved. This includes avoiding them having to repeat information, having to repeatedly contact the company, switching channels, being transferred, and being treated in a generic manner."[3]

Part of the solution is eliminating the archaic way customer service representatives are managed. As explained in *The Effortless Experience*, you can empower "frontline reps to deliver a low-effort experience by using incentive systems that value the quality of the experience over merely speed and efficiency. They've moved away from the 'stopwatch' and 'checklist' culture that's long permeated the service organization to instead give reps more autonomy and the opportunity to exercise a greater degree of judgment. They understand, in other words, that to get greater control over the quality of the experience delivered, they need to give greater control to the people delivering it."[4]

Speed of time and speed of service are critical to your customer experience. Everyone in the organization has to understand how valuable time is to the customer. Companies like Google, Zappos, and Amazon have absorbed

> The world of the internet has made everything instantaneous, from information to products in people's hands . . . This has also changed customers' ability to be patient. They now expect not only phone calls and emails returned the same day, within an hour, but also support and resolutions to problematic issues.

this lesson and shaped your customers' expectations. The world of the internet has made everything instantaneous, from information to products in people's hands. Today a friend can recommend a good book, and within 30 seconds it is in your hands on your Kindle. You can order a product and companies may have it at your door the same day. This has also changed customers' ability to be patient. They now expect not only phone calls and emails returned the same day, within an hour, but also support and resolutions to problematic issues.

## Consumers Are Buying Time

Whether it is due to the hours we put into our careers or the constant demands of rushing from one child's activities to the next, being time poor has increased the stress on many adults. No surprise, then, that some of the fastest-growing new businesses are those that sell services instead of products, specifically time-saving services. They say you can't buy time, but today's consumers are using their disposable income to do just that. An article published by the Proceedings of the National Academy of Sciences shows that those who spend money on timesaving services actually feel happier.[5]

There is a wide range of services one can buy to get more time back. They include help with household chores (cleaning, cooking, repairs, and landscaping) and car services so you can be productive on your commute to work. There is also pickup and drop-off for car maintenance or dry cleaning, virtual assistants, and online shopping and dog walkers. You can arrange for personal chefs, restaurant delivery services like Uber Eats, or order healthy prepared food, ready to be cooked, from companies like Blue Apron. There is seemingly no end to what you can outsource today or in the future. We have gone from do-it-yourself to "do-it-for-me" (DIFM).

"[These consumers] prioritize spending time with their kids or their hobbies over mowing the yard, cleaning the house, or washing their cars," says Scot Wingo, cofounder of ChannelAdvisor and CEO of Spiffy, an on-demand car-care service. "Importantly, the DIFM consumer is willing to spend money to save time. In the next five years, I think it will feel as archaic as using the Yellow Pages to have to 'call' a service provider. Your phone will be the remote control for your life, and you will have a myriad of products and services available to you at your whim in a completely transparent and digital way."[6]

> In the next five years, I think it will feel as archaic as using the Yellow Pages to have to "call" a service provider. Your phone will be the remote control for your life, and you will have a myriad of products and services available to you at your whim in a completely transparent and digital way.

The ease of doing business just got easier. Amazon's Dash button allows consumers to order products like more shampoo or dog food by Wi-Fi, by pressing the button in your home. Even easier, products and groceries now show up at people's businesses or homes automatically, without someone placing an order. Smart printers automatically order ink when levels get low, and washing machines order detergent after a certain number of cycles. While consumers shop, they can look at an app on their smartphones, which is communicating with their refrigerators and freezers, to see what products they are low on. Smart fridges notify customers when food reaches an expiration date; eventually it will reorder your Miller Lite because you have only four bottles left.

## The Retail Renaissance

A decade ago, it appeared that brick-and-mortar retailers were on the way to extinction. Sales were shifting to e-commerce and physical stores were closing at an epic rate. Most people didn't expect the retail pendulum to shift again. However, what was originally brick and mortar became click and order and has now evolved to clicks and mortar—a combination of in-store and online shopping. Even Amazon and Google have opened up brick-and-mortar stores. Why? Because those companies realize that it is hard to build an emotional connection with a strictly online presence in today's Relationship Economy.

Amazon has gone a step further in its physical stores by eliminating traditional customer pain points: no more waiting in lines. It feels like shoplifting. You walk in, grab whatever you want, and walk out. It is that easy and simple. Best of all, it is legal!

The brand's no-cash/no-cashier stores are called Amazon Go. This checkout-free shopping experience is backed by Amazon's "Just Walk Out" technology, which features overhead cameras, weight sensors, and deep learning technology that can detect merchandise that shoppers take from or return to shelves, and keep track of items selected in a virtual cart. Shoppers use the Amazon Go mobile app to gain entry to the store through a turnstile. When customers leave the store, the Just Walk Out technology automatically debits their Amazon account for the items they have chosen and then sends a receipt to the app. As a side benefit, this sophisticated technology has virtually eliminated shoplifting, which according to the National Retail Federation drains some $47 billion from retailers nationwide each year.[7]

## ExperienTAIL = Experience + Retail

Some retailers have figured out the importance of staging a true shopping experience and relationship building by combining entertainment and emotional engagement. Best Buy has embraced the showroom model. For the digitally inclined, it supplies real-life virtual reality. CNBC called the company "a retail anomaly" because it's actually fun to shop there; kids get to sample video games and adults get to play with the latest gadgets. The appeal has translated to business success. Best Buy's stock rose more than 20 percent in 2017 after the company's in-store sales soared past expectation.[8]

> Retailers have figured out the importance of staging a true shopping experience and relationship building by combining entertainment and emotional engagement.

As a wonderland for gadget-geeks, Best Buy has also worked with partners like Google and Samsung to establish small sections of the store where each can show off new products. Visit a Samsung area, for example, and you'll find the latest smartphones and tablets, virtual-reality headsets, and accessories. In the gaming section you can try out high-end mechanical keyboards, super-accurate mice, and fancy gaming headsets with surround-sound audio. Shoppers crave these kinds of places, where they can go to see, feel, and play with the products.[9]

Entertainment plus emotional engagement has long been part of the dining experience. I hate letting my kids choose where we go to dinner, because I know they'll opt for our local Japanese steakhouse. Places like Benihana have been extremely successful for decades. These restaurants have created a cult following by staging theatrical dining. Unlike most restaurants, the chef is the entertainment here and makes you part of the show. Kids can be mesmerized by an onion volcano. Mom can enter the act by trying to catch a piece of airborne broccoli in her mouth.

In "Why All New Businesses Need to Think Like a Benihana Chef," Ryan Williams says, "Benihana's appeal is more about community—the shared experience of watching a cook make your meal right in front of you. This collaborative experience is atypical . . . As modern entrepreneurs or professionals in the digital age, you need to 'cook' with and collaborate with your customers."[10]

The trend has been taken on by some movie theaters, which have been dramatically hurt by DIRECTV, Amazon, and Netflix. For over a decade, ticket sales have been on the decline in the United States. So progressive movie theaters are now offering gourmet dining, alcohol, and servers who bring it all to you as you settle into your comfy reclining seats.

Brian Schultz, the founder and CEO of the Studio Movie Grill chain, which pioneered the in-theater dining concept, points out that he believes hospitality trumps bells and whistles when it comes to the new way of moviegoing. "Give the guest an exceptional experience. All the amenities mentioned will not be productive or produce a great guest experience without hospitality and service," he says.[11]

## The Willy Wonka of Coffee

For the past three decades, Starbucks has set the standard for what a coffee experience should be, demonstrating how it was possible to make the price of coffee irrelevant. Now the company has launched a new chain called Starbucks Reserve. "We recognize our customers expect and desire a higher level of product, and we want to give it to them," says former CEO Howard Schultz, who in 2017 stepped down from that role to focus full time on the new Reserve concept.[12]

This is not your typical grab-and-go latte place. The Reserve stores are significantly larger than the typical Starbucks stores, and an order of coffee there could easily cost $12. Think of it like a coffee "winery." The baristas turn the ritual of grabbing a cup of coffee into a well-orchestrated experience. They prepare small-batch coffee using specific methods like siphon brewing. They also offer coffee flights and cold-brew floats. Once again Schultz's incredible vision goes against conventional wisdom.

> I have talked for a year now about this seismic change of consumer behavior changing and going away from bricks and mortar traditional retail shopping and to ecommerce and mobile. In order to mitigate that, I think it's incumbent upon the responsibility of retailers to create these fantastic experiences [that are] going to sweep them away.

Schultz says, "This majestic place will take our customers on a magical carpet ride. Nine and a half years ago I wrote in a journal, let's create the Willy Wonka of Coffee. I wanted to create this multi-sensory experience with theatre, romance, drama and have the coffee moving around and create a real roasting manufacturing facility and we have done it."

He adds, "I have talked for a year now about this seismic change of consumer behavior changing and going away from bricks and mortar traditional retail shopping and to ecommerce and mobile. In order to mitigate that, I think it's incumbent upon the responsibility of retailers to create these fantastic experiences [that are] going to sweep them away."[13]

## Loyalty to a Common Purpose

In "Marketing Revolution: The Rise of the Relationship Economy," Tom LaForge, Coca-Cola's former global director of human and cultural insights, talks about how marketers unintentionally commoditized their products to the point that consumers' loyalty has dramatically decreased. As a result of losing market share, marketers were forced to stop focusing on the products' functional and emotional benefits and highlight their social attributes instead.[14]

"Social attributes are about relationships," says LaForge. "It is this universality and consistency that has more and more marketers and manufacturers layering social attributes on top of existing products or using them as the foundation for new ones. When a person decides to buy a product for its social attributes, they're making a statement about what they believe a good relationship is. These are values-based statements. And values are rock solid foundations upon which brand loyalty can reside for a long, long time. Social attributes make declarations like, products should be made in a way that nurtures humankind's relationship with the planet. Communities should thrive along with the companies doing business within their borders. And corporations must care and act for the wellbeing of others as they do their own."[15]

LaForge points out the impact social attributes can have when they are connected to products like shoes or a soft drink. "They lift that product from a sea of banal sameness in which price is the primary differentiator to a

> They lift that product from a sea of banal sameness in which price is the primary differentiator to a place where meaning and values decrease the differentiating power of price. This is a place where the buying decision feels more rewarding, more purposeful.

place where meaning and values decrease the differentiating power of price." He concludes, "This is a place where the buying decision feels more rewarding, more purposeful. It's a place where loyalty regains some of its strength because it is a new kind of loyalty—not loyalty to a brand, but the feeling one feels for those dedicated to the same higher purpose as they are. Brands that share our dedication to a cause greater than ourselves and provide a mechanism for collective action will thrive."[16]

His comments are particularly important when considering millennials as consumers.

## This Is Not Your Parents' Bank

Where can you go to chill out for as long as you want, grab a latte, enjoy free Wi-Fi, connect with others, snack on a pastry, and have access to community iPads? You probably said Starbucks. I should add that you can also receive complimentary financial coaching. Would you believe you could get all of this at a bank? Times are indeed changing, and the traditional banking model is going the way of the dinosaur.

Let me introduce you to Capital One Café, which is part of an effort to win over what is now the largest segment of the US workforce—millennials. A vast majority of the 35-and-younger population have boycotted the traditional banking experience; they bank strictly online.[17]

Financial advisors, known as Capital One "ambassadors" (many of them certified life coaches) offer workshops on various topics such as financing a wedding and how to talk to your spouse about money. As for sipping while you ponder your bank account, Capital One has partnered with Peet's Coffee to provide beverages and snacks for purchase in each café. While you don't have to be an existing customer to stop in for refreshment, Capital One cardholders receive 50 percent off any drink purchase. These cafés also offer large conference rooms for local businesses and charities to use free of charge.

## Millennials: Money Is Made for Memories

In the same vein, a study by the Harris Group reveals that 72 percent of millennials prefer to spend their hard-earned cash on experiences rather than on material goods. This generation cares less about cars and houses and more about skydiving and touring foreign countries. It's a trend that has ultimately helped fuel the growth of billion-dollar-plus start-ups like Uber, WeWork, and Airbnb. Millennials—who have tremendous spending power that will continue to accelerate—want more than products and services for their money. Experiential moments and exceptional customer service are key to earning their loyalty and stimulating a positive social response. Unfortunately many retailers haven't adjusted to this trend. Be forewarned: Those who don't adapt will cease to exist.[18]

"Millennials aren't spending our money on cars, TVs, and watches," Taylor Smith, CEO and co-founder of

> This generation cares less about cars and houses and more about skydiving and touring foreign countries.

> Experiential moments and exceptional customer service are key to earning their loyalty and stimulating a positive social response. Unfortunately many retailers haven't adjusted to this trend. Be forewarned: Those who don't adapt will cease to exist.

Blueboard, told CNBC. "We're renting scooters and touring Vietnam, rocking out at music festivals, or hiking Machu Picchu." Smith has applied that concept to businesses; Blueboard sells "experiential" packages to companies, designing perks such as skydiving, cooking classes, and couples massages.[19]

## Intentional Attention Builds Fanatical Loyalty

Relationship, entertainment, experiences, and a larger purpose—all these elements come together in Peloton, which has created an incredibly passionate, loyal customer base. A Peloton bike is a high-end, new-age stationary bike with a virtual screen. According to Neen James, author of *Attention Pays: How to Drive Profitability, Productivity, and Accountability,* "Peloton knows their riders want lifestyle changes, so they created a technology company that helps people achieve their goals and packaged it in a fun, sexy bike . . . a bike that goes nowhere! Customers can ride spin bikes either in the company's New York studio, or they purchase Peloton brand bikes for use in their homes."

James continues, "John Foley, the CEO, knows the value of relationships between his customers and his instructors. He will tell you Peloton is a technology company that has paid attention to every touch point for riders, instructors, and visitors to the New York studio and boutique. Every interaction, online, offline and in person is designed to engage the community. They pay attention to all the little details to build relationships with their customers."

Peloton instructors know they will build a bigger and more engaged community by regularly giving shout-outs to riders by name. They also celebrate milestone rides, that is, 50, 100, and 500 rides.

This personal touch keeps riders coming back and wanting to achieve the next level of fitness and earn recognition badges.

"The community (100,000-plus riders strong) on Peloton's private Facebook page has been one of the most interesting insights of my Peloton purchase," notes James. "They are like a cult, obsessed with rides, health and even the instructors—in the most positive way. Peloton has created a fun tribe of strangers who hold each other accountable and cheer each other on."

Peloton has grown faster than Facebook, Apple, and Google in the past four years. How do you measure their success? At the time of writing, they were valued at more than $1.25 billion dollars and growing fast.[20]

## Don't Sleep on the Boomers

Amid all the fanfare and buzz around millennials, it is important not to lose sight of the buying power and resources of the more mature consumer. The 74.9 million baby boomers still represent a huge chunk of the US population; in fact, the millennial population is only a touch larger at 75.9 million.[21] What's interesting about baby boomers, however, is that they have the disposable income to spend on what they want—something many millennials don't yet have because of their age, income, and the rising cost of living. According to an article in *Bloomberg Technology*, millennials will spend more than $200 billion annually, and $10 trillion during their lifetimes. But the spending power of baby boomers is predicted to be $15 trillion worldwide annually.[22]

> *"The most important component of a world-class experience is that the staff is not focused on selling stuff. They are focused on building relationships and trying to make people's lives better."*

## CHAPTER 9 TAKEAWAYS

- Your competitor has the same products and services that you do. So all things being equal, how can an organization tip the scale in its favor? Convenience.

- If you want to win in business, figure out how to be more convenient than your competition by removing traditional bottlenecks that customers are sick of.

- The key to mitigating disloyalty is reducing customer effort. Companies should focus on making service easier, not more delightful, by reducing the amount of work required of customers to get their issues resolved.

- Train customer-facing reps to deliver a low-effort experience by using incentive systems that value the quality of the experience over mere speed and efficiency.

- The world of the internet has made everything instantaneous, from information to products in people's hands. This has also changed customers' ability to be patient. They now expect not only phone calls and emails returned the same day, within an hour, but also support and resolutions to problematic issues.

- The fastest-growing new businesses are those that sell time-saving services. They say you can't buy time, but today's consumers are using their disposable income to do just that.

- ExperienTAIL = Experience + Retail

- Retailers have figured out the importance of staging a true shopping experience and building relationships by combining entertainment and emotional engagement.

- Seventy-two percent of millennials prefer to spend their hard-earned cash on experiences rather than on material goods. This generation cares less about cars and houses and more about skydiving and touring foreign countries.

- Experiential moments and exceptional customer service are key to earning millennials' loyalty and stimulating positive social responses. Unfortunately many retailers haven't adjusted to this trend. Be forewarned: Those who don't adapt will cease to exist.

- The spending power of baby boomers is predicted to be $15 trillion worldwide *annually*.

# CARPE MOMENTO

> *"We are at our best when creating enduring relationships and personal connections. When we are fully engaged, we connect with, laugh with, and uplift the lives of our customers—even if it is just for a few moments. It's really about human connection."*
>
> —HOWARD SCHULTZ, STARBUCKS[1]

*Carpe momento*—"seize the moment." And there's no better motto for reminding us that any connection with others—especially building relationships—depends on being fully engaged with them. When you are with others, BE THERE. Be around your family, friends, and coworkers. Be there for someone, and let someone be there for you. There's a reason we're called human beings and not human doings. At the end of the day, ask yourself one simple question: "How many people had a better day as a result of coming in contact with me?"

> At the end of the day, ask yourself one simple question: "How many people had a better day as a result of coming in contact with me?"

According to a study conducted by psychologists at Harvard University, adults spend only 50 percent of their time in the present moment. That means we are mentally checked out half of the time. Scientists also found that when we are in the present moment, we are at our happiest, no matter what we are doing.[2]

One of the leading predictors of success and happiness is developing strong relationships. And one of the best ways to improve your ability to connect with others on a more meaningful level is learning to be present, which makes the people around you feel understood, valued, and supported.

> *"Obsessing about the past and worrying about the future rips us out of the only place where we can find true happiness: the present moment."*

## Customer Loyalty Comes From Micro-Experiences

Too many customer-facing employees are convinced that customers will be happy and loyal if they get the results they were hoping for when doing business with them. That's not true. Think about it. If you have a toothache, don't you expect the dentist, any dentist, to fix it? If you go to a high-end steakhouse and order your filet mignon medium rare and it comes out medium rare, do you do backflips? If the package you ordered arrives within two days as promised, are you wowed? And if your accounting firm prepares your tax returns accurately and the IRS does not audit you, are you impressed? Not at all; that is what you are paying for when you deal with reputable businesses. However, if that is all you get, there is a high probability you will not be a loyal customer. Why? You would have received those results from any of those company's viable competitors.

Customer loyalty is a result of the multiple positive micro-experiences a person has with a brand. It reflects the fact that not only is that business consistently brilliant at the basics, but also that it has taught all its employees to be present in the moment at each of its touch points.

We need to educate and change the mind-set our employees have regarding what drives customers' loyalty. The outcome by itself does not make customers loyal, but I am not talking about adding fancy bells and whistles or blow-your-socks-off, above-and-beyond acts. I am talking about simple, executable experiences that can be delivered in every customer interaction.

> Too many customer-facing employees are convinced that customers will be happy and loyal if they get the results they were hoping for when doing business with them. That's not true. Customer loyalty is a result of the multiple positive micro-experiences a person has with a brand.

Here are some examples of positive micro-experiences: A receptionist greets a patient by name when she arrives for an appointment; or a waiter remembers what you ordered the last time you were in. Or your customer service rep contacts you to let you know they are out of stock on one of the products you ordered, but that he tracked the product down from another distributor so you would have enough to get you through the end of the month. Or perhaps your consultant sends you a book on how to train for your first marathon, because she remembered a conversation you two had last week. Each of these examples will have a major impact on customer retention.

> *Our focus must be providing a positive experience*
> *on EVERY interaction, whether it is face-to-face,*
> *click-to-click, or ear-to-ear.*

## URX

Today, too many companies think they are in a race to evolve their customer experience from costly human interactions to technology like self-check-in/out, apps, kiosks, social media, and online support. While these represent a necessary evolution for most business models, we must not send the message to our employees that success is no longer about them and what they do. That will make our employees feel less important or have a decreased sense of value and disconnection from the company's purpose, which will create employee apathy. Employee apathy produces customer apathy. Employee apathy is a sign of a terminally ill business. We cannot let our leaders and employees rely on technology as a crutch for the customer experience.

> Employee apathy produces customer apathy. Employee apathy is a sign of a terminally ill business.

Our employees need to be reminded constantly that "You are the eXperience" (URX). It is about them and how they interact with the customer. Apps, iPads, websites, and kiosks don't build relationships. People do. Employees who connect, instead of just communicate, create loyal customers.

Sven Gierlinger, vice president and

> Never lose sight of the impact you make on other people in any given moment. The choice you make to smile (or not), to follow through (or not), to be empathetic (or not) makes a bigger difference than you will ever know.

chief experience officer of Northwell Health, inspires his staff by reminding them, "Every moment that we come into contact with our patients and customers matters. Never lose sight of the impact you make on other people in any given moment. The choice you make to smile (or not), to follow through (or not), to be empathetic (or not) makes a bigger difference than you will ever know. Choose wisely."[3]

## Five Ways Your Customer Experience Is Always on Stage

Your employees need to understand that they are always on stage, whether they are interacting directly with the customer or not. Each interaction has an impact on the experience your customer perceives. Labeling your customer experience "Always on Stage" is a way to help your entire organization realize how their actions are seen through their customer's eyes. Here are five examples of ways your experience is always on stage:

### 1. Leave it at the door.

Always be aware of how you act when you are dealing with customers, regardless of what you have going on in your life. This includes not over-sharing about work, personal life, slow computers,

> The client is paying for their experience—not yours. Leave yours at the door.

or blaming coworkers for problems. It also includes avoiding the dreaded RBF syndrome. The best customer service employees are Academy Award–winning actors or actresses at times.

## 2.  You are still on stage.

Employees sometimes forget that they are still on stage when they are not directly dealing with customers, but customers can still see or hear them. This could be employees or receptionists talking to each other about their personal life, making negative comments about other customers, or complaining about their job, all within earshot of a customer who may be in the waiting area. This could also be an employee reading text messages or eating in front of customers when they are off the clock. The customer doesn't know the employee is off the clock. All they see is an unprofessional employee.

## 3.  Must be present to win.

If you are really present with a customer, a firecracker could go off nearby and you wouldn't even realize it. Employees need to understand how unprofessional it is to have personal conversations with coworkers while engaging with a customer or multitasking while on a call. The greatest gift you can give someone is your undivided attention.

> If you are really present with a customer, a firecracker could go off nearby and you wouldn't even realize it.

## 4.  Everyone is your customer.

The experience you deliver extends far beyond customers. It is how you act and treat coworkers, vendors, people you buy from, even strangers in an elevator. World-class service is not something you do or deliver; it is something that is in you, in all areas of your life.

## 5.  Everyone is in the media.

In the past, there were journalists who reported stories of interest on television, on radio, and in newspapers. Today every single person with access to a smartphone with a camera and social media is a reporter. Businesses need to make significant changes in the experience they deliver, since customers can share their level of satisfaction with your company on sites like Yelp, Facebook, Twitter, and Instagram. Today every business is one experience away from going viral. Remember the United Airlines staff members dragging a passenger off a flight or two African American men arrested at Starbucks in Philadelphia because they hadn't ordered anything? These stories would never have made the headlines 20 years ago. However, today anyone with a smartphone can catch companies mistreating customers and then post the video.

## All About Energy

Energy attracts people like nothing else. People love energy. Energy is about a vibe, a person's spirit, and the fire they have inside of them. Motivational speaker Mel Robbins says it best: "Your energy introduces you before you even speak."

> Your energy introduces you before you even speak.

Think about the favorite places you like to hang out. Do you want to walk into a restaurant, bar, or salon with barely anyone inside and employees standing around bored? No way! When that happens, people sometimes say there is a "lack of atmosphere." What's really missing is energy. We love energy— the hustle and bustle of positive movement. When you walk into an Apple Store, you can feel the energy. It is everywhere, people are interacting, playing with products, learning, being educated. This also applies to individuals. We need to focus on the energy we are bringing into a room and into every interaction.

> *"Beauty is energy. It is about how you show up in the world,*
> *what do you bring, what is unique about you."*
> —GRACE KILLELEA

## THERE YOU ARE!

If you have ever seen the movie *Jerry Maguire*, there is the epic scene where Tom Cruise's character returns to try to win over Renee Zellweger with a long-winded speech. Zellweger interrupts him and says the famous line, "You had me at hello." Whether it be in business or personal, do you have people at hello? The best way to greet someone is with the expression, "There you are!" Not necessarily with those words, but with that meaning or expression. Speaker Christine Cashen says, "Greet people like they are your favorite person, make others feel good about who they are."

> The best way to greet someone is with the expression, "There you are!" Greet people like they are your favorite person, make others feel good about who they are.

A great role-playing scenario we like to do in our training sessions is to have two employees get up in front of the room. One of them has to act as if they bumped into a good friend from high school (the other employee) whom they haven't seen in several years. What would that look like, how would they react? They always do a double take with the expression, "There you are!" That results in a natural and authentic execution of the five Es: enthusiastic greeting, eye contact, ear-to-ear smile, engagement, and education about their life since they last saw each other. (See chapter 6 for more about the five Es.)

You can express "There you are!" in many ways—face-to-face, over the phone, or in an email. We have all heard someone who sounds excited to be talking to us, and it's obvious in emails, too.

As I mentioned earlier, The DiJulius Group works with NewDay USA, a mortgage company serving veterans and their families, based in Fulton, Maryland, and headed by retired Admiral Thomas Lynch. On one of my early visits to the NewDay USA offices, someone asked me if I wanted to pop my head into Admiral Lynch's office and say hello. "Of course," I said, since I had only met him briefly. As I was brought into his office, he was seated at his desk reading what appeared to be a report. When he looked up and saw me, he literally threw that report up in the air and said, "Holy cow! It is John DiJulius." The papers flew up like confetti. I was shocked.

Never before had I had such a greeting. I felt like a true VIP and walked away with a bounce in my step. Then it hit me: If one of the highest-ranking officers in the US Navy could make me feel that way, why couldn't I give that type of welcome to more people? My employees, my clients, even my kids deserve that when I see them. It made me want to provide a positive, energizing moment with everyone I come in contact with. And the way I can do that is by greeting people with the expression, "THERE YOU ARE!"

> *"You serve others by being engagingly present."*

Most interactions in our day are simple chitchat, focused around the weather, our most recent trip, or what we did over the weekend.

However, research has proven small talk does not build relationships nor is it great for our levels of happiness.

## Screw Small Talk, Go for Big Talk

As a student at Northwestern University, Kalina Silverman performed a social experiment for a research project and ended up starting a global movement called Big Talk. Due to her own struggles with loneliness in college, Silverman wanted to be able to meet new people, skip the small talk, and instead have deeper conversations and make more meaningful connections. She began by filming a video series in which she approached strangers and skipped the small talk to ask them, "What do you want to do before you die?" These total strangers shocked her. "I was surprised when people not only shared with me their deepest desires but told me many moving life stories as well," says Silverman. "Some of these conversations with initial strangers turned into friendships I still maintain today. Inspired by my experiences making 'Big Talk,' I wanted to share what I learned with others. So I edited the footage into a video I posted to YouTube."[4]

> I thought about how many amazing moments and relationships we could be experiencing if we incorporated big talk more in our interactions.

After the video went viral and was picked up by the *Huffington Post* and *USA Today*, the Big Talk movement was born. I encourage you to watch Kalina Silverman's TEDx Talk on "How to Skip the Small Talk and Connect with Anyone," which has more than 5 million views.[5]

Watching that video made me think about how often we waste meaningful opportunities every day by making small talk. I thought about how many amazing moments and relationships we could be experiencing if we incorporated Big Talk more in our interactions with coworkers, customers, friends, and even strangers. As a result I have a list of Big Talk questions stored on my smartphone for times when the situation calls for going deep. Here are some of my Big Talk questions:

- Who would you love to have lunch with?
- What do you want do before you die?
- If you found out you were going to die tomorrow, what would you do today?
- If you died today, what would have been your biggest regret?
- What achievement from your childhood are you most proud of?
- What keeps you up at night?
- Who do/did you respect the most in life and why?
- If you could change one thing in your life right now, what would it be?
- What was the biggest obstacle you have had to overcome?
- Who are the top five people you have ever met and why?
- Who is your favorite celebrity and why?
- What do you think you could have done better at?
- What is the best thing you received from either of your parents?
- How is your child like you in the most positive way?
- How is your child like you in the most negative way?
- If your life were a book, what would be the title of the chapter you are living right now?

- Other than marriage and birth of children, what was the best day of your life?
- If you retired today, what would be the biggest regret of your career?
- What are three things I would be shocked to know about you?

I personally have used Big Talk on leadership retreats with my own organizations. Many of the answers were surprising. Several people got emotional. Most important, even though many of us have known each other and worked closely together for more than 10 years, we found out a lot more about each other.

Think about how you can use Big Talk more in your own life, as a business leader with your team members, customers, and vendors. Also, think about how you can use it in your personal life with your significant other, children, and friends. I promise you will be shocked at the deeper conversations and connections you will enjoy.

## Strangers Are Friends You Haven't Met Yet

Strangers are where our greatest opportunities lie—they're future connections, friendships, resources, experiences, laughs, and good times. Or maybe just a familiar face to smile and nod at the next time your paths cross. Some people are placed in our life for a specific reason or we were placed in their life at a critical time. Decide today that there are no such things as strangers, just amazing people you haven't met yet.

# What a 13-Year-Old Can Teach Us About Customer Service

I have had the good fortune to witness many professionals who truly know how to build an emotional connection with others. However, one person in particular consistently blows me away with how well he builds rapport instantly with strangers and learns so much about other people in only a few minutes of conversation. This person is my youngest son, Bo DiJulius. I have been intrigued by his ability to strike up a conversation with someone he has never met before and have the other person, usually an adult, share so much about themselves with a young teenager. So I asked Bo if he would share how he does it. The following is a blog post that Bo wrote on his own customer service philosophy when he was 13 years old.

### *Making People Feel Like They Are the Real Deal*[6]
#### By Bo DiJulius

Some businesses don't look at customer service the way it should be. It just makes life easier for so many people, including yourself.

Treat customers like a celebrity and make them feel special. Make them want to come back. Why do I do this? Well, I just love that feeling when you know someone is going home with a smile. You help that somebody and also yourself, because positivity is just as contagious as negativity. So, fill the air with joy and bright smiles.

> I just love that feeling when you know someone is going home with a smile.

I will give you an example. I was at the Cheesecake Factory in Buffalo, New York, eating with my dad. A couple was sitting at a table next to us. While my dad got up and went to the bathroom, I decided to stop playing Pokémon Go on my phone and said, "Where are you guys from?" The woman was from Germany and the man was from Buffalo. They were dating too. I learned so much as we spoke, and it was one of the craziest things ever.

John Stanz was the man's name. He served 10 years in the Marines as a staff sergeant. He was shot in the ear one time and also blown up in a truck by an I.E.D. He broke and tore so many things I can't remember. He was in a coma for 5 1/2 weeks. His family was called out to say their goodbyes because John had a 0 percent chance of living. His family said NO they will not give up. His parents were forced to quit their jobs. Amazingly John woke up from his coma but was told that he would never be able to speak, eat on his own, or walk ever again. Almost two years went by, and John has recovered and has overcome the impossible. He still has lots of injuries but is a hero.

> The thing is what if I didn't say, "Where are you guys from?" I could have missed out on something that inspired me so much.

The thing is what if I didn't say, "Where are you guys from?" I could have missed out on something that inspired me so much. That's why you have to talk and learn and meet people. Thank you for your time and remember, make people feel like they are the real deal so you can be the real deal. If you ever want to contact me, then email me at bodijulius9@gmail.com, bodijulius on Twitter and Instagram. You'll find the kid who is learning and living an amazing life thanks to my amazing father and two brothers who taught me it all. Thank you and have a great day.

*"Shut off the past and ignore the future. We are living our lives only when we focus on the moments of each day. When we focus on being in the moment, in seizing each moment, and wringing out all life has, the days, weeks, months, and years take care of themselves. Decide today to live in the moment, make each moment count in your life and the lives of those you value."*

## CHAPTER 10 TAKEAWAYS

- Carpe momento—"seize the moment."

- Adults spend only 50 percent of their time in the present moment.

- Customer loyalty comes from micro-experiences.

- Too many customer-facing employees are convinced that customers will be happy and loyal if they get the results they were hoping for when doing business with them. That's not true.

- Our focus must be providing a positive experience on EVERY interaction, whether it is face-to-face, click-to-click, or ear-to-ear.

- URX—You are the eXperience.

- Technology doesn't build relationships, people do. Employees who connect, instead of just communicate, create loyal customers.

- Five ways your customer experience is always on stage:

  1. Leave it at the door.

  2. You are still on stage.

3. Must be present to win.

4. Everyone is your customer.

5. Everyone is in the media.

- Your energy introduces you before you even speak.
- The best way to greet someone is with the expression, "There you are!"
- Greet people like they are your favorite person; make others feel good about who they are.
- Screw small talk, go for Big Talk.
- Make people feel like they are the real deal.

# GIVE MORE

*"We have to have a sense of urgency to do what we were born to do, to make an impact, and leave a legacy. Our time is very short, shorter than any of us realize."*

I have never been a collector of objects. I'm not too nostalgic about things, at least not anything physical. However, I realize that I have collected something very special and priceless my entire life. People actually compliment me on my collection all the time. I constantly stress to my three sons and all my employees that they should collect the same things I do, since I believe what I collect is the best gauge of a person's character.

What I collect are relationships with rare people. The key word is "rare," for I am extremely choosy. I collect relationships with uncommon, loyal, unique, highly moral, genuine, and, most importantly, POSITIVE people.

> I collect relationships with rare people. I collect relationships with uncommon, loyal, unique, highly moral, genuine, and, most importantly, POSITIVE people.

> *"If I am judged by the people I surround myself with,*
> *I am a champion."*

## No One Succeeds Alone

I attribute 100 percent of my success to the collection of relationships I have, from my closest friends, mentors, managing partners, leaders in my businesses, long-term employees, and customers who have become more than just business associates to family members, my sons, and my significant other. Every one of them embodies the qualities of the list above. I want to be guilty by association.

Whether you ran a marathon, competed in an ironman, built a multimillion-dollar business from the ground up, found a cure for cancer, ended poverty, or created world peace, you didn't do it alone. It is important to recognize that you had help every step of the way. All our accomplishments are the result of hundreds of contributions throughout our lives. Many we remember, many we don't, because most affected us subconsciously. These moments affected our minds, our character, why we think the way we do, why we work so hard, why we are OCD about certain things, and why we have the will to never quit and never give up.

You are the average of the five people you spend the most time with. If that statement bothers you, do something about it, both personally and professionally. It is important to recognize the contributions of others. They may be the leading cast members in our life—our parents, friends, coaches, teachers, bosses, siblings, significant others, coworkers, vendors, customers, and employees. There are also many invisible support characters in our journey of success: trainers, assistant coaches, janitors, neighbors, babysitters, people from our community, and casual acquaintances. Remember the people who believed in you before you believed in yourself.

I know for me personally the only reason why I accomplished certain things earlier in my life was because I didn't have the heart to let down people who believed in me. Remember those who gave you a second (and third and fourth) chance, allowed you to screw up, and gave you the opportunity to make it right.

> **Remember those who gave you a second (and third and fourth) chance, allowed you to screw up, and gave you the opportunity to make it right.**

## No Such Thing as a "Self-Made Man"

I have the greatest job ever. When I am fortunate enough to get a standing ovation after a presentation, I wish my team could be on stage with me basking in that ovation. It takes a lot of people behind the scenes to make me look good. My amazing support team helped the client choose me for their event and took care of the logistics, prep work, scheduling, flights, and hotels. The team does their job so well that it allows me to focus on creating content and better deliver a customized presentation for a particular audience. I am also supported by an incredible nanny who takes care of my boys and my house while I travel. It doesn't seem fair that I am the one on stage enjoying an audience's ovation, when so many others deserve the credit.

Marketing innovator Ekaterina Walter wrote in her blog that "Everything in life is built on relationships. There is no such thing as a 'self-made man.' And if anyone tells you otherwise, that person doesn't understand the power of partnerships, the power of network, the power of generosity."[1]

> *"You'll be left with an empty feeling if you hit the finish line alone. It is much more rewarding when you cross the finish line as a team. Don't forget about the people who helped you, pushed you, and believed in you."*

Everyone you spend time with influences you, either negatively or positively. True friends are those who really know you but who love you anyway. Life is relationships, the rest is just details. The most important aspect of life is focusing on building relationships and trying to make people's lives better.

## We Are Just Tourists

The sooner each of us realize we are just tourists on earth, we will live more in the moment. We are just temporary visitors here, and our passports can expire at any time. Nothing is guaranteed—our time, our kid's time, not anyone's time. Life isn't about what is fair or unfair. If we focus on today and stop wasting the time we have with others as if it were unlimited, we will have so much less regret. Carpe momento!

> Nothing is guaranteed—our time, our kid's time, not anyone's time. Life isn't about what is fair or unfair. If we focus on today and stop wasting the time we have with others as if it were unlimited, we will have so much less regret. Carpe momento!

## To Live—The Ultimate Experience

ALWAYS DISCOVER AND LEARN—TAKE RISKS, FAIL OFTEN, PERSEVERE RELENTLESSLY, AND SUCCEED—FIND YOUR PASSION, YOUR NICHE—SHARE AND TEACH—BUILD AMAZING RELATIONSHIPS, LOVE, FEEL EMOTIONS, BE VULNERABLE, EXPERIENCE LOSS AND JOY—CARE AND SHOW KINDNESS—CONSTANTLY APPRECIATE AND SHOW GRATITUDE—WE MUST BUILD, INNOVATE, AND CREATE OPPORTUNITY—ALWAYS GIVE MORE AND LEAVE THINGS BETTER AS A RESULT OF YOUR PRESENCE.

## Give More

The best way to build long-term sustainable relationships is to give more in both your personal life and in business. I have tried to build my life's purpose around these two words—give more.

We live in a very cynical society. We tend to operate by agreement: You do A, B, and C, and I do X, Y, and Z. However most people wait to make sure the other person does their part first. What I try to practice and teach my employees and my boys is do X, Y, and Z first and throw in W, even though it wasn't part of the deal. Give *more* than the deal says, *more* than what is expected. Don't wait for the other person to do what they promised, don't keep score, and don't have a good memory. Don't remember three years ago when someone didn't do what he or she said. If you borrow your neighbor's pickup truck to move furniture, return it cleaner and with more gas than it had originally.

> If you borrow your neighbor's pickup truck to move furniture, return it cleaner and with more gas than it had originally.

Just give more.

> "To *build meaningful relationships, I invite you to Give More in all your relationships.*"

## CHAPTER 11 TAKEAWAYS

- Collect relationships with rare people. Collect relationships with uncommon, loyal, unique, highly moral, genuine, and, most importantly, POSITIVE people. Be guilty by association.

- Remember those who gave you a second (and third and fourth) chance, allowed you to screw up, and gave you the opportunity to make it right.

- There's no such thing as a "self-made man."

- Nothing is guaranteed—our time, our kid's time, not anyone's time. Life isn't about what is fair or unfair. If we focus on today and stop wasting the time we have with others as if it were unlimited, we will have so much less regret. Carpe momento!

- Give more in every relationship.

- If you borrow your neighbor's pickup truck to move furniture, return it cleaner and with more gas than it had originally.

- To build meaningful relationships, I invite you to *give more* in all your relationships.

# NOTES

## Chapter 1

1. Simon Sinek, "Millennials in the Workplace," YouTube, https://www.youtube.com/watch?v+5MC2X-LRbkE.

2. Nick Nauert, "How Meaningful Relationships Can Help Us Thrive," PsychCentral, August 8, 2018, https://psychcentral.com/news/2014/09/01/involvement-in-a-meaningful-relationship-brings-out-the-best-in-a-person/74388.html.

3. Laura Trowbridge, "Study: Lack of Friends Is Like Smoking 15 Cigs a Day Health Wise," *Digital Journal*, August 7, 2010. http://www.digitaljournal.com/article/295653.

4. Ed Yong, "The Incredible Thing We Do During Conversations," *The Atlantic*, January 4, 2016, https://www.theatlantic.com/science/archive/2016/01/the-incredible-thing-we-do-during-conversations/422439/.

5. Ben Healy, "How to Make Friends, According to Science," *The Atlantic*, September 2018, https://www.theatlantic.com/magazine/archive/2018/09/how-to-make-friends/565742/.

6. Susan Scott Berkley, *Fierce Conversations: Achieving Success at Work and in Life One Conversation at a Time*, (New York: Penguin Random House, 2004).

7. Ben Healy, "How to Make Friends, According to Science," *The Atlantic*, September 2018, https://www.theatlantic.com/magazine/archive/2018/09/how-to-make-friends/565742/.

8. "A Better Way to Measure and Value Business Relationships," The Relational Capital Group, April 2010, http://www.relationalcapitalgroup.com/downloads/EnterpriseRQ-whitepaper.pdf.

## Chapter 2

1. Dan Schawbel, *Back to Human: How Great Leaders Create Connection in the Age of Isolation,* (New York: Da Capo Press, 2018).

2. Tom Peters, *The Excellence Dividend: Meeting the Tech Tide with Work That Wows and Jobs That Last,* (New York: Vintage Books, 2018).

3. Saheli Roy Choudhury, "A.I. and Robotics Will Create Almost 60 Million More Jobs than They Destroy by 2022, Report Says," *CNBC*, September 17, 2018, https://www.cnbc.com/2018/09/17/wef-machines-are-going-to-perform-more-tasks-than-humans-by-2025.html.

4. Tom Peters, *The Excellence Dividend: Meeting the Tech Tide with Work That Wows and Jobs That Last,* (New York: Vintage Books, 2018).

5. Jonathan Maze, "Is Spyce The Future of the Restaurant Business?" *Restaurant Business*, September 10, 2018, https://www.restaurantbusinessonline.com/financing/spyce-future-restaurant-business.

6. Chris Albrecht, "Haidilao and Panasonic Team Up for Robotic Hotpot Restaurant," *The Spoon*, October 25, 2018, https://thespoon.tech/haidilao-and-panasonic-team-up-for-robotic-hotpot-restaurant/.

7. Danny Paez, "Google Duplex A.I. Turned Smartphones Into Reservation-Making Assistants," *Inverse*, December 26, 2018, https://www.inverse.com/article/52023-google-duplex-turned-smartphones-into-ai-secretaries.

8. "AI Will Power 95 Percent of Customer Interactions by 2025," *AI Business* (blog), March 10, 2017, https://aibusiness.com/ai-will-power-95-of-customer-interactions-by-2025/.

9. Clint Boulton, "Why Bots Are Poised to Disrupt the Enterprise," *CIO*, September 28, 2016, https://www.cio.com/article/3124638/it-industry/why-bots-are-poised-to-disrupt-the-enterprise.html.

10. "Chatbot Conversations to Deliver $8 Billion in Cost Savings by 2022," *Juniper Research*, July 24, 2017, https://www.juniperresearch.com/analystxpress/july-2017/chatbot-conversations-to-deliver-8bn-cost-saving.

11. Bill Fischer, "The End of Expertise," *Harvard Business Review*, October 19, 2015, https://hbr.org/2015/10/the-end-of-expertise?utm_medium=referral&utm_source=pulsenews.

12. Erik Brynjolfsson and Andrew McAfee, *Race Against the Machine: How the*

*Digital Revolution Is Accelerating Innovation, Driving Productivity, and Irreversibly Transforming Employment and the Economy* (Self-pub, 2011).

13. Brian Halligan, "Replacing the Sales Funnel with the Sales Flywheel," *Harvard Business Review*, November 20, 2018, https://hbr.org/2018/11/replacing-the-sales-funnel-with-the-sales-flywheel.

14. Luke Brynley-Jones, "Can Online Customer Service Deliver a Higher ROI than Marketing?" *Our Social Times*, http://oursocialtimes.com/can-customer-service-deliver-a-higher-roi-than-marketing/.

15. "The ROI from Marketing to Existing Online Customers," Adobe Digital Index, 2012, https://success.adobe.com/assets/en/downloads/whitepaper/13926.digital_index_loyal_shoppers_report.pdf.

16. Scott Magids, Alan Zorfas, and Daniel Leemon, "What Separates the Best Customers from the Merely Satisfied," *Harvard Business Review*, December 3, 2015, https://hbr.org/2015/12/what-separates-the-best-customers-from-the-merely-satisfied.

17. "Customer Experience Management (CEM) Market Size, Share & Trends Analysis Report by Analytical Tool, by Touch Point Type (Call Centers, Mobile, Email, Social Media), by Deployment, by End-User, and Segment Forecasts, 2018 – 2025," *Grand View Research*, May 2018, https://www.grandviewresearch.com/industry-analysis/customer-experience-management-market.

18. "The Business Impact Of Investing In Experience," Forrester Consulting, April 2018, https://wwwimages2.adobe.com/content/dam/acom/en/experience-cloud/research/roi/pdfs/business-impact-of-cx.pdf.

## Chapter 3

1. Leo Sun, "Facebook Inc's Chatbots Hit a 70% Failure Rate," *The Motley Fool*, February 28, 2017, https://www.fool.com/investing/2017/02/28/facebook-incs-chatbots-hit-a-70-failure-rate.aspx.

2. Eivind Jonassen, "The Impact of AI and the Empathy Economy on the Customer Experience," *Omnicus*, August 28, 2018, https://blog.omnicus.com/the-impact-of-ai-and-the-empathy-economy-on-the-customer-service-experience.

3. Kristin Smaby, "Being Human Is Good Business," *A List Apart*, September 6, 2011, http://alistapart.com/article/being-human-is-good-business.

4. Joshua Feast, "The Empathy Economy: Emotional Intelligence in Customer Service," *Xconomy*, July 5, 2018, https://xconomy.com/boston/2018/07/05/the-empathy-economy-emotional-intelligence-in-customer-service/.

5. Richard R. Shapiro, *The Endangered Customer: 8 Steps to Guarantee Repeat Business*, (New Jersey: The Center for Client Retention, 2016).

6. Richard R. Shapiro, *The Endangered Customer: 8 Steps to Guarantee Repeat Business*, (New Jersey: The Center for Client Retention, 2016).

7. Juergen Tolksdorf, "Driving Customer Experience through the Agent Experience," *Genesys*, November 30, 2017, https://www.genesys.com/blog/post/driving-customer-experience-through-the-agent-experience.

8. Roger Simpson, "Surviving and Thriving in an Amazon World," LinkedIn, February 25, 2018, https://www.linkedin.com/pulse/surviving-thriving-amazon-world-roger-simpson/.

9. Rima Qureshi, Doug Manuel, Chip Conley, Meagan Fallone, Fadi Chehade, Bryn Freedman, Gary Cohen, and Ruby Sales, "TED Salon: Humanizing our Future," TED, September 20, 2018, https://tedlive.ted.com/webcasts/TEDSalon20180920; Roger Simpson, "Surviving and Thriving in an Amazon World," LinkedIn, February 25, 2018, https://www.linkedin.com/pulse/surviving-thriving-amazon-world-roger-simpson/.

10. Roger Simpson, "Surviving and Thriving in an Amazon World," LinkedIn, February 25, 2018, https://www.linkedin.com/pulse/surviving-thriving-amazon-world-roger-simpson/.

11. Simone Stolzoff, "LinkedIn CEO Jeff Weiner Says the Biggest Skills Gap in the US is Not Coding," *Quartz at Work*, October 15, 2018, https://qz.com/work/1423267/linkedin-ceo-jeff-weiner-the-main-us-skills-gap-is-not-coding/.

12. Carmine Gallo, *Five Stars: The Communication Secrets to Get from Good to Great,* (New York: St. Martin's Press, 2018).

13. Kate Taylor, "Chick-fil-A Is Beating Every Competitor by Training Workers to say 'Please' and 'Thank You,'" *Business Insider*, April 16, 2017, http://www.businessinsider.com/chick-fil-a-is-the-most-polite-chain-2017-4.

14. Kate Taylor, "Chick-fil-A Is Beating Every Competitor by Training Workers to

say 'Please' and 'Thank You,'" *Business Insider*, April 16, 2017, http://www.businessinsider.com/chick-fil-a-is-the-most-polite-chain-2017-4.

15. "Best Service at Fast Food Restaurants in America," *Consumer Reports*, July 2014, http://www.consumerreports.org/cro/magazine/2014/08/best-service-at-fast-food-restaurants-in-america/index.htm.

16. Jareen Imam, "'Resting Bitch Face' Is Real, Scientists Say," *CNN*, February 4, 2016, http://www.cnn.com/2016/02/03/health/resting-bitch-face-research-irpt/.

17. Roger Highfield, Richard Wiseman, and Rob Jenkins, "How Your Looks Betray Your Personality," *New Scientist*, February 11, 2009, https://www.newscientist.com/article/mg20126957.300-how-your-looks-betray-your-personality/?full=true.

18. Richard Branson, "Talk Less—Smile More," Virgin, https://www.virgin.com/richard-branson/talk-less-smile-more.

## Chapter 4

1. "Digital Dementia and 7 Tips to Avoid It," *Nontoxic Living*, August 9, 2017, https://www.nontoxicliving.tips/blog/digital-dementia-what-it-is-7-tips-to-avoid-it.

2. Dan Schawbel, *Back to Human: How Great Leaders Create Connection in the Age of Isolation,* (New York: Da Capo Press, 2018).

3. Dan Schawbel, *Back to Human: How Great Leaders Create Connection in the Age of Isolation,* (New York: Da Capo Press, 2018).

4. Craig Bloem, "84 Percent of People Trust Online Reviews As Much As Friends. Here's How to Manage What They See," *Inc.*, July 31, 2017, https://www.inc.com/craig-bloem/84-percent-of-people-trust-online-reviews-as-much-.html.

5. Chris Morran, "Congress Asks Airline Industry to Explain Why It 'Hates the American People,'" *Consumerist*, May 9, 2017, https://consumerist.com/2017/05/02/congress-asks-airline-industry-to-explain-why-it-hates-american-people/.

6. "Digital Dementia and 7 Tips to Avoid It," *Nontoxic Living*,

August 9, 2017, https://www.nontoxicliving.tips/blog/
digital-dementia-what-it-is-7-tips-to-avoid-it.

7. "Digital Dementia and 7 Tips to Avoid It," *Nontoxic Living*,
   August 9, 2017, https://www.nontoxicliving.tips/blog/
   digital-dementia-what-it-is-7-tips-to-avoid-it.

8. Carlos Vidaurreta, *Digital Dementia*, (2018; YouTube), Video, https://www.
   youtube.com/watch?v=TB5imNoNVmQ&t=10s.

9. Elizabeth Segran, "What Really Happens to Your Brain
   and Body During a Digital Detox," *Fast Company*,
   July 30, 2015, https://www.fastcompany.com/3049138/
   what-really-happens-to-your-brain-and-body-during-a-digital-detox.

10. Manoush Zomorodi, *How Boredom Can Lead to Your Most Brilliant Ideas*,
    (2017; TED2017), Video, https://www.ted.com/talks/manoush_zomorodi_
    how_boredom_can_lead_to_your_most_brilliant_ideas?utm_campaign=ios-
    share&utm_medium=social&source=email&utm_source=email.

11. Manoush Zomorodi, *How Boredom Can Lead to Your Most Brilliant Ideas*,
    (2017; TED2017), Video, https://www.ted.com/talks/manoush_zomorodi_
    how_boredom_can_lead_to_your_most_brilliant_ideas?utm_campaign=ios-
    share&utm_medium=social&source=email&utm_source=email.

12. Manoush Zomorodi, *How Boredom Can Lead to Your Most Brilliant Ideas*,
    (2017; TED2017), Video, https://www.ted.com/talks/manoush_zomorodi_
    how_boredom_can_lead_to_your_most_brilliant_ideas?utm_campaign=ios-
    share&utm_medium=social&source=email&utm_source=email.

13. David Crossman, *Simon Sinek on Millennials in the Workplace*, performed
    by Simon Sinek, (2016; YouTube), Video, https://www.youtube.com/
    watch?v=hER0Qp6QJNU&app=desktop.

14. David Crossman, *Simon Sinek on Millennials in the Workplace*, performed
    by Simon Sinek, (2016; YouTube), Video, https://www.youtube.com/
    watch?v=hER0Qp6QJNU&app=desktop.

15. Tripp Mickle, "Apple Unveils Ways to Help Limit iPhone Usage,"
    *Wall Street Journal*, June 4, 2018, https://www.wsj.com/amp/articles/
    apple-unveils-ways-to-help-limit-iphone-usage-1528138570.

16. Elizabeth Segran, "What Really Happens to Your Brain
    and Body During a Digital Detox," *Fast Company*,
    July 30, 2015, https://www.fastcompany.com/3049138/
    what-really-happens-to-your-brain-and-body-during-a-digital-detox.

17. Elizabeth Segran, "What Really Happens to Your Brain and Body During a Digital Detox," *Fast Company*, July 30, 2015, https://www.fastcompany.com/3049138/ what-really-happens-to-your-brain-and-body-during-a-digital-detox.

18. Elizabeth Segran, "What Really Happens to Your Brain and Body During a Digital Detox," *Fast Company*, July 30, 2015, https://www.fastcompany.com/3049138/ what-really-happens-to-your-brain-and-body-during-a-digital-detox.

19. Gary Turk, *Look Up*, (2014; YouTube), Video, https://www.youtube.com /watch?v=Z7dLU6fk9QY.

20. Gary Turk, *Look Up*, (2014; YouTube), Video, https://www.youtube.com /watch?v=Z7dLU6fk9QY.

## Chapter 5

1. Ed Yong, "The Incredible Thing We Do During Conversations," *The Atlantic*, January 4, 2016, https://www.theatlantic.com/science/archive/2016/01/ the-incredible-thing-we-do-during-conversations/422439/.

2. Rich Simmonds, "The ART of Listening . . . Leading and Selling," Rich Simmonds, May 7, 2015, http://richsimmondsza.com/2015/05/07/ the-art-of-listening-leading-and-selling/.

3. Rich Simmonds, "The ART of Listening . . . Leading and Selling," Rich Simmonds, May 7, 2015, http://richsimmondsza.com/2015/05/07/ the-art-of-listening-leading-and-selling/.

4. Tom Peters, *The Excellence Dividend: Meeting the Tech Tide with Work That Wows and Jobs That Last*, (New York: Vintage Books, 2018).

5. Tom Peters, *The Excellence Dividend: Meeting the Tech Tide with Work That Wows and Jobs That Last*, (New York: Vintage Books, 2018).

6. Tom Peters, *The Excellence Dividend: Meeting the Tech Tide with Work That Wows and Jobs That Last*, (New York: Vintage Books, 2018).

7. Jack Zenger and Joseph Folkman, "What Great Listeners Actually Do," *Harvard Business Review*, July 14, 2016, https://hbr.org/2016/07/ what-great-listeners-actually-do.

8. Jack Zenger and Joseph Folkman, "What Great Listeners Actually Do," *Harvard Business Review*, July 14, 2016, https://hbr.org/2016/07 /what-great-listeners-actually-do.

9. Jack Zenger and Joseph Folkman, "What Great Listeners Actually Do," *Harvard Business Review*, July 14, 2016, https://hbr.org/2016/07/what-great-listeners-actually-do.

10. Susan Scott Berkley, *Fierce Conversations: Achieving Success at Work and in Life One Conversation at a Time*, (New York: Penguin Random House, 2004).

11. Tom Peters, *The Excellence Dividend: Meeting the Tech Tide with Work That Wows and Jobs That Last*, (New York: Vintage Books, 2018).

12. Tom Peters, *The Excellence Dividend: Meeting the Tech Tide with Work That Wows and Jobs That Last*, (New York: Vintage Books, 2018).

13. Jessica Stillman, "3 Habits That Will Increase Your Empathy," *Inc.*, August 22, 2014, https://www.inc.com/jessica-stillman/3-habits-that-will-increase-your-empathy.html.

14. Scott Gerber and Ryan Paugh, *Superconnector: Stop Networking and Start Building Business Relationships that Matter*, (New York: Da Capo Press, 2018).

15. Jack Zenger and Joseph Folkman, "What Great Listeners Actually Do, *Harvard Business Review*, July 14, 2016, https://hbr.org/2016/07/what-great-listeners-actually-do.

16. Jessica Stillman, "3 Habits That Will Increase Your Empathy," *Inc.*, August 22, 2014, https://www.inc.com/jessica-stillman/3-habits-that-will-increase-your-empathy.html.

## Chapter 6

1. "A Better Way to Measure and Value Business Relationships," The Relational Capital Group, April 2010, http://www.relationalcapitalgroup.com/downloads/EnterpriseRQ-whitepaper.pdf.

2. CEO Coaching International, *Sheldon Wolitski on Going From a $12,000 Credit Card Cash Advance to $110 Million in Revenue*, (SoundCloud), Podcast, http://ceocoachinginternational.com/sheldon-wolitski-going-12000-credit-card-cash-advance-110-million-revenue/.

3. Verne Harnish, *Scaling Up: How a Few Companies Make It . . . and Why the Rest Don't (Rockefeller Habits 2.0)*, (Virginia: Gazelles Inc., 2014).

4. Verne Harnish, *Scaling Up: How a Few Companies Make It . . . and Why the Rest Don't (Rockefeller Habits 2.0)*, (Virginia: Gazelles Inc., 2014).

5. "What We Do," Cedar Brook Financial Partners, LLC, https://www.cedarbrookfinancial.com/what-we-do.aspx.

6. Jane Cobler, email message to author, August 7, 2018.

7. Stephen Bruce, "Dan Pink: To Sell, Make It Personal," HR Daily Advisor, July 29, 2013, http://hrdailyadvisor.blr.com/2013/07/29/dan-pink-to-sell-make-it-personal/#.

8. Adam Bryant, "Walt Bettinger of Charles Schwab: You've Got to Open Up to Move Up," *The New York Times*, February 4, 2016, https://www.nytimes.com/2016/02/07/business/walt-bettinger-of-charles-schwab-youve-got-to-open-up-to-move-up.html.

9. Matthew Dixon, Nick Toman, and Rick Delisi, *The Effortless Experience: Conquering the New Battleground for Customer Loyalty,* (New York: Penguin Group, 2013).

10. Keith Ferrazzi and Tahl Raz, *Never Eat Alone: And Other Secrets to Success, One Relationship at a Time,* (New York: Crown, 2005).

11. Keith Ferrazzi and Tahl Raz, *Never Eat Alone: And Other Secrets to Success, One Relationship at a Time,* (New York: Crown, 2005), 366.

## Chapter 7

1. Mark Cuban, *How to Win at the Sport of Business: If I Can Do It, You Can Do It,* (New York: Diversion Books, 2011).

2. John R. DiJulius III, *Secret Service: Hidden Systems That Deliver Unforgettable Customer Service*, (New York: AMACOM, 2003), 46–48.

3. David Maister, "A Matter of Trust," David Maister, 1998, https://davidmaister.com/articles/a-matter-of-trust/.

4. Lewis Howes, *The School of Greatness: A Real-World Guide to Living Bigger, Loving Deeper, and Leaving a Legacy.*

5. Scott Gerber and Ryan Paugh, *Superconnector: Stop Networking and Start Building Business Relationships that Matter*, (New York: Da Capo Press, 2018).

6. Jeff Shore, "Don't Wage a Price War. Win Sales by Eliminating Your

Competition," *Entrepreneur*, September 2, 2014, http://www.entrepreneur.com/article/236990.

7. Susan Scott Berkley, *Fierce Conversations: Achieving Success at Work and in Life One Conversation at a Time*, (New York: Penguin Random House, 2004).

8. Matthew Dixon, Nick Toman, and Rick Delisi, *The Effortless Experience: Conquering the New Battleground for Customer Loyalty*, (New York: Penguin Group, 2013).

9. Darren Hardy, *The Compound Effect: Jumpstart Your Income, Your Life, Your Success*, (New York: Vanguard Press, 2011).

10. Darren Hardy, *The Compound Effect: Jumpstart Your Income, Your Life, Your Success*, (New York: Vanguard Press, 2011).

11. Darren Hardy, *The Compound Effect: Jumpstart Your Income, Your Life, Your Success*, (New York: Vanguard Press, 2011).

12. Darren Hardy, *The Compound Effect: Jumpstart Your Income, Your Life, Your Success*, (New York: Vanguard Press, 2011).

13. Seth Godin, "Instead of Outthinking the Competition . . ." Seth's Blog, September 30, 2012, https://seths.blog/2012/09/instead-of-outthinking-the-competition/.

## Chapter 8

1. Admiral Thomas Lynch, email message to author, July 17, 2018.

2. "ABC (Always Be Connecting)," Robin Sharma, https://www.robinsharma.com/article/abc-always-be-connecting.

3. Family and Work Institute, as quoted in www.kenblanchard.com/ignite/ignite_volume7_2005.html.

4. http://gmj.gallup.com/gmj_surveys, as quoted in The Ken Blanchard Companies, www.kenblanchard.com/ignite/ignite_volume7_2005.html.

5. Rob Markey, "The Four Secrets to Employee Engagement," *Harvard Business Review*, January 27, 2014, http://blogs.hbr.org/2014/01/the-four-secrets-to-employee-engagement/.

6. Rob Markey, "The Four Secrets to Employee Engagement," *Harvard Business Review*, January 27, 2014, http://blogs.hbr.org/2014/01/the-four-secrets-to-employee-engagement/.

7. "State of the American Workplace," 2017, https://news.gallup.com /reports/178514/state-american-workplace.aspx.

8. Kevin Freiberg and Jackie Freiberg, "20 Reasons Why Herb Kelleher was one of the Most Beloved Leaders of Our Time," *Forbes*, January 4, 2019, https://www.forbes.com/sites/kevinandjackiefreiberg/2019/01/04/20-reasons-why-herb-kelleher-was-one-of-the-most-beloved-leaders-of-our-time/#179d33e5b311.

9. Jonathan Meyer, email message to author, June 15, 2018.

10. Donna Cutting, *501 Ways to Roll Out the Red Carpet for Your Customers*, (New Jersey: Career Press, 2015).

11. Daniel H. Pink, *When: The Scientific Secrets of Perfect Timing*, (New York: Riverhead Books, 2018).

12. Daniel H. Pink, *When: The Scientific Secrets of Perfect Timing*, (New York: Riverhead Books, 2018).

13. David Horsager, "You Can't Be a Great Leader Without Trust—Here's How You Build It," *Forbes*, October 24, 2012, https://www.forbes.com/sites/ forbesleadershipforum/2012/10/24/you-cant-be-a-great-leader-without-trust-heres-how-you-build-it/#cc34c234ef7a.

14. David Horsager, "You Can't Be a Great Leader Without Trust—Here's How You Build It," *Forbes*, October 24, 2012, https://www.forbes.com/sites/ forbesleadershipforum/2012/10/24/you-cant-be-a-great-leader-without-trust-heres-how-you-build-it/#cc34c234ef7a.

15. David Horsager, "You Can't Be a Great Leader Without Trust—Here's How You Build It," *Forbes*, October 24, 2012, https://www.forbes.com/sites/ forbesleadershipforum/2012/10/24/you-cant-be-a-great-leader-without-trust-heres-how-you-build-it/#cc34c234ef7a.

16. Donna Cutting, *501 Ways to Roll Out the Red Carpet for Your Customers*, (New Jersey: Career Press, 2015).

17. Donna Cutting, *501 Ways to Roll Out the Red Carpet for Your Customers*, (New Jersey: Career Press, 2015).

18. Donna Cutting, *501 Ways to Roll Out the Red Carpet for Your Customers*, (New Jersey: Career Press, 2015).

19. John Ruhlin, *Giftology: The Art and Science of Using Gifts to Cut Through the Noise, Increase Referrals, and Strengthen Client Retention*, (Self-pub, 2016).

20. Daniel H. Pink, *When: The Scientific Secrets of Perfect Timing*, (New York: Riverhead Books, 2018).

21. Adam Bryant, "Walt Bettinger of Charles Schwab: You've Got to Open Up to Move Up," *The New York Times*, February 4, 2016, https://www.nytimes.com/2016/02/07/business/walt-bettinger-of-charles-schwab-youve-got-to-open-up-to-move-up.html.

22. Arnie Malham, *Worth Doing Wrong: The Quest to Build a Culture That Rocks*, (South Carolina: Advantage, 2016).

23. Kenneth H. Blanchard, *The One-Minute Manager*, (New York City: William Morrow, 2003).

24. Jeff Toister, "The Outsized Impact of Invisible Service Providers," Toister Performance Solutions, Inc., October 24, 2017, https://www.toistersolutions.com/blog/2017/10/17/the-outsized-impact-of-invisible-service-providers.

25. Simon Sinek, *Leaders Eat Last: Why Some Teams Pull Together and Others Don't*, (New York: Penguin Random House, 2017).

## Chapter 9

1. Kristi Garced, "Hugo Boss Unveils Boss on Demand," WWD, July 29, 2016, https://wwd.com/fashion-news/fashion-scoops/hugo-boss-on-demand-shopping-10498755/.

2. Matthew Dixon, Nick Toman, and Rick Delisi, *The Effortless Experience: Conquering the New Battleground for Customer Loyalty*, (New York: Penguin Group, 2013).

3. Matthew Dixon, Nick Toman, and Rick Delisi, *The Effortless Experience: Conquering the New Battleground for Customer Loyalty*, (New York: Penguin Group, 2013).

4. Matthew Dixon, Nick Toman, and Rick Delisi, *The Effortless Experience: Conquering the New Battleground for Customer Loyalty*, (New York: Penguin Group, 2013).

5. Ashley V. Whillans, Elizabeth W. Dunn, Paul Smeets, Rene Bekkers, and Michael I. Norton, "Buying Time Promotes Happiness," *PNAS*, July 24, 2017, http://www.pnas.org/content/114/32/8523.full.

6. Andrew Medal, "Forget That Product You're Working On. What's Really

Going to Sell in the Future Is . . . Service," *Entrepreneur*, April 20, 2018, https://www.entrepreneur.com/article/312243.

7. Matt McFarland, "I Spent 53 Minutes in Amazon Go and saw the Future of Retail," *CNN*, October 3, 2018, https://www.cnn.com/2018/10/03/tech /amazon-go/index.html.

8. Todd Haselton, "How Best Buy Escaped the Retail Apocalypse," CNBC, May 25, 2017, https://www.cnbc.com/2017/05/25/why-best-buy-shares-are-up. html; Brian Halligan, "Replacing the Sales Funnel with the Sales Flywheel," *Harvard Business Review*, November 20, 2018, https://hbr.org/2018/11/ replacing-the-sales-funnel-with-the-sales-flywheel.

9. Todd Haselton, "How Best Buy Escaped the Retail Apocalypse," CNBC, May 25, 2017, https://www.cnbc.com/2017/05/25/why-best-buy-shares-are-up. html; Brian Halligan, "Replacing the Sales Funnel with the Sales Flywheel," *Harvard Business Review*, November 20, 2018, https://hbr.org/2018/11/ replacing-the-sales-funnel-with-the-sales-flywheel.

10. Ryan Williams, "Why All New Businesses Need to Think Like a Benihana Chef," *Observer*, October 10, 2016, http://observer.com/2016/10/ why-all-new-businesses-need-to-think-like-a-benihana-chef/.

11. Bob Strauss, "With More Alcohol, Gourmet Food and Plush Seats, Movie Theaters add Luxuries to Bring in Customers," *Los Angeles Daily News*, May 13, 2018, https://www.dailynews.com/2018/05/13/with-more-alcohol-and- plush-seating-are-socal-movie-theater-upgrades-working-the-proof-may-be-in- the-pudding/.

12. Chris Isidore, "Starbucks Plans New Upscale Chains," *CNN*, July 14, 2016, https://money.cnn.com/2016/07/14/news/companies/starbucks-upscale-chain/ index.html.

13. Chris Isidore, "Starbucks Plans New Upscale Chains," *CNN*, July 14, 2016, https://money.cnn.com/2016/07/14/news/companies/starbucks-upscale-chain/ index.html.

14. Tom LaForge, "Marketing Revolution: The Rise of the Relationship Economy," *The Guardian*, October 9, 2013, https://www.theguardian.com/ sustainable-business/social-impact-brand.

15. Tom LaForge, "Marketing Revolution: The Rise of the Relationship Economy," *The Guardian*, October 9, 2013, https://www.theguardian.com /sustainable-business/social-impact-brand.

16. Tom LaForge, "Marketing Revolution: The Rise of the Relationship Economy," *The Guardian*, October 9, 2013, https://www.theguardian.com/sustainable-business/social-impact-brand.

17. Tanza Loudenback, "Capital One Is Trying to Curry Favor with Millennials with Cafés Around the US Offering Free Wi-Fi, Local Coffee and Food, and Complimentary Money Coaching," *Business Insider*, February 9, 2017, https://www.businessinsider.com/inside-capital-one-cafe-for-millennials-2017-2.

18. Uptin Saiidi, "Millennials Are Prioritizing 'Experiences' Over Stuff," *CNBC*, May 5, 2016, http://www.cnbc.com/2016/05/05/millennials-are-prioritizing-experiences-over-stuff.html.

19. Uptin Saiidi, "Millennials Are Prioritizing 'Experiences' Over Stuff," *CNBC*, May 5, 2016, http://www.cnbc.com/2016/05/05/millennials-are-prioritizing-experiences-over-stuff.html.

20. Emily Cohn, "A Billion-Dollar Fitness Startup that Came out of Nowhere Could Kill SoulCycle," *Business Insider*, May 25, 2017, http://www.businessinsider.com/peloton-is-now-worth-more-than-1-billion-2017-5.

21. Richard Fry, "Millennials Project to Overtake Baby Boomers as America's Largest Generation," *Pew Research Center*, March 1, 2018, http://www.pewresearch.org/fact-tank/2016/04/25/millennials-overtake-baby-boomers/.

22. Matthew Boyle, "Aging Boomers Stump Marketers Eyeing $15 Trillion Prize," *Bloomberg*, September 16, 2013, https://www.bloomberg.com/news/articles/2013-09-17/aging-boomers-befuddle-marketers-eying-15-trillion-prize.

**Chapter 10**

1. Howard Schultz and Joanne Gordon, *Onward: How Starbucks Fought for Its Life without Losing Its Soul,* (New York: Rodale Books, 2011.

2. Emma Seppälä, "6 Secrets to a Happier Life," *Time*, August 7, 2017, http://time.com/4856944/secrets-happier-life/.

3. Donna Cutting, *501 Ways to Roll Out the Red Carpet for Your Customers*, (New Jersey: Career Press, 2015).

4. TEDx Talks, *How to Skip the Small Talk and Connect with Anyone*, performed by Kalina Silverman, (2016; YouTube), Video, https://www.youtube.com/watch?v=WDbxqM4Oy15.

5.  TEDx Talks, *How to Skip the Small Talk and Connect with Anyone*, performed by Kalina Silverman, (2016; YouTube), Video, https://www.youtube.com/watch?v=WDbxqM4Oy16.

6.  John R. DiJulius III, "Customer Service from a 13 Year Old," The DiJulius Group, September 8, 2016, https://thedijuliusgroup.com/what-a-13-year-old-can-teach-us-about-customer-service/.

## Chapter 11

1.  Ekaterina Walter, "There Is No Such Thing as a Self-Made Man," Ekaterina Walter, February 25, 2014, http://www.ekaterinawalter.com/there-is-no-such-thing-as-a-self-made-man/.

# INDEX

# ABOUT THE AUTHOR

As the authority on world-class customer experience, John DiJulius is sought by organizations across the world wanting to use his philosophies and methodology for creating world-class service. He has worked with companies such as The Ritz-Carlton, Lexus, Starbucks, Nestle, Marriott Hotel, PWC, Celebrity Cruises, Progressive Insurance, Chick-fil-A, and many more to help them continue to raise the bar and set the standard in service that consistently exceeds customer expectations.

John is the president of The DiJulius Group, a customer service consulting firm whose purpose is to change the world by creating a customer service revolution. He founded his first business in 1993—John Robert's Spa, an upscale chain (with more than 150 employees)—which has been named one of the top 20 salons in America. John is also the founder of Believe in Dreams, a nonprofit that fulfills dreams of economically disadvantaged youth who suffer from severe hardship. John resides in Aurora, Ohio, with his three boys, Johnni, Cal, and Bo.